Mr. Callahan is Associate Professor of Classics and Philosophy at Georgetown University.

# FOUR VIEWS OF TIME
# IN ANCIENT PHILOSOPHY

LONDON : GEOFFREY CUMBERLEGE
OXFORD UNIVERSITY PRESS

# FOUR VIEWS
# OF TIME
# ·IN·
# ANCIENT
# PHILOSOPHY

*John F. Callahan*

HARVARD UNIVERSITY PRESS

*Cambridge*

1948

PRINTED AT THE HARVARD UNIVERSITY PRINTING OFFICE
CAMBRIDGE, MASSACHUSETTS, U.S.A.

PARENTIBVS · MEIS · SACRVM

# *Preface*

THE PROBLEM of time, one of the most important in the history of philosophy, has been treated by philosophers of every age in many different ways. It is not surprising that it receives careful consideration from the four men who might well be thought the outstanding philosophers of the ancient world. But what is very striking is that each of the four philosophers considers the problem of time from an entirely different point of view. Each in his own way has made a contribution that not only in itself is highly constructive but has also been of great influence in the subsequent history of philosophy. Solutions of the problem of time are still proposed that go back in their essentials to one of these four ancient views, even though the modern philosopher may be unaware that his theory is not being offered for the first time. It would be difficult, moreover, to find four modern analyses of time that, taken together, throw as much light on this interesting problem as do these ancient views.

It seems strange, then, that these four theories of time, which supplement one another in a most unusual way, have not received more consideration, especially insofar as they can be contrasted from the standpoint of philosophical method. Surely the different approaches of these four philosophers to the problem of time are not unrelated both to their views of reality as a whole and to the method of philosophical analysis that each believes most proper to the discovery of truth.

There are many difficulties that beset the person who attempts to interpret a problem of this kind as it appears in four great philosophers, and this treatise does not pretend to have met all or even most of these difficulties successfully. It should be noted that many of the problems involving time have had to be omitted in order to avoid going too far astray from the main purpose of this study. The best mode of procedure seemed to be to follow the analysis of the philosopher himself and see at first hand the close relationship between his method and his discovery of an acceptable theory of time. This procedure involves paraphrase and commentary, with shorter or longer interspersed discussions of the interrelations of the various philosophers. Although this sometimes involves considerable detail, which it has often been tempting to omit, the detail seemed to be an intrinsic part of the philosopher's study and therefore worthy of inclusion. References are given constantly so that it is possible for the reader to follow the text of the philosopher if he wishes to do so.

I am deeply indebted to Professor Richard McKeon, of the University of Chicago, who originally suggested the problem of time as worthy of study with reference to various philosophic methods, and provided both inspiration and concrete assistance at all stages of the work. I also wish to thank Professor Werner Jaeger, of Harvard University, both for the scholarly counsel that he has constantly offered and for the encouragement that he has given toward the actual publication of the book. In addition, the Harvard Institute for Classical Studies, of which he is the Director, has generously aided the publication of this volume by a financial subsidy. Professor Berthold L. Ullman, of the University of North Carolina, kindly read an earlier draft and made many helpful suggestions with regard to clarity of expression. The defects that remain are to be ascribed to the author alone.

I wish to acknowledge with thanks the permission granted by the Oxford University Press to quote from two of its publications.

Finally, my thanks are due to the staff of the Harvard University Press for their expert and conscientious handling of all the details of publication.

J. F. C.

GEORGETOWN UNIVERSITY
Washington, D. C.
May, 1948

# Contents

# FOUR VIEWS OF TIME
# IN ANCIENT PHILOSOPHY

# I

# PLATO

## *Time, the Moving Image of Eternity*

IN APPROACHING the problem of time as it is set forth by Plato, the first Greek philosopher to discuss it at length, we must first examine the *Timaeus* and begin by summarizing the discussion leading up to the entrance of time into the dialogue. Such a summary must be relatively long in the case of Plato because Plato does not define time for us, but rather speaks of it in terms of analogies and metaphors, so that we tend to miss its various aspects if we do not keep the entire context in mind. For Plato asks us first to survey the entire plan of the universe, a universe which he constructs with his dialectic and sets forth as the framework within which the meaning of time is to be understood; he then asks us to grasp the significance of time by observing the relationship it possesses to the other beings within this universe.

### THE ORIGIN OF THE UNIVERSE

In our dialectical construction of the universe in the *Timaeus* we first of all consider whether the universe has come into existence or is without becoming (27c). This question leads us to distinguish two realms that will later have a direct bearing on time, being and becoming, that which always is and never becomes, and that which always becomes and never is. The former is apprehended by thought together with a definition, whereas the latter is conjectured by opinion together with perception but without a definition. Plato now states the principle that everything that becomes must have a cause of its becoming, though for Plato this is less a principle, at least as Taylor, for example, understands it to be a principle,[1] than it is a generalization from experience. On the basis of this generalization we are able to set up a craftsman for the universe, who is conceived on the analogy of a human craftsman, and to see what light such an analogy throws on the universe. We can say that any craftsman who takes as his model the everlasting, changeless being produces necessarily a fair work, but the one who takes a created model produces one that is not fair. Plato thus insists that any work of art that is fair must embody a form or meaning that is unchanging, even though the embodiment itself may or may not continue to exist.

We now return to the original question: did the universe exist forever, having no principle of becoming, or has it come into being, beginning from some principle? Timaeus in the dialogue answers that the universe has come into being, for he again generalizes by saying that everything that is visible, tangible, and corporeal, like the universe, has come into existence. All such things are sensible, and sensible things, apprehended by opinion together with perception, are things that come into being. Thus we place the universe on the side of becoming as opposed to being, recalling our previous distinction, and we say that the universe is always

---

[1] A. E. Taylor, *A Commentary on Plato's Timaeus* (Oxford: The Clarendon Press, 1928), p. 63.

becoming. Since it is always coming into existence we find that we are justified in saying that it has a cause, just as the things that come into existence in the realm of art have a cause. But can we interpret this "coming to be" of the universe to mean that it had a first moment of existence, or is it eternally produced? This question must be considered later in the light of subsequent passages in the dialogue.

Carrying farther the analogy of the craftsman, we ask whether the maker of this universe had an unchanging model or a created one. If the universe is fair and the craftsman good, then he took as his model the eternal. But the universe is the fairest of created things and he is the best of causes. The universe, therefore, has an eternal, unchanging model. When we speak of the model which is unchanging, our discourse should be itself unchanging and irrefutable, as far as any discourse can be that (Plato does not expect anything compounded of words to preserve its meaning perfectly). But the discourse that pertains to the image should have a probability that is in a certain proportion to the truth of the other discourse: as being is to becoming, so truth is to belief. In speaking of the universe's becoming and of the gods, we must be satisfied with a probable account. Plato repeats this caution elsewhere in the dialogue,[2] and since he looks upon words as being untrustworthy,[3] we shall more easily perceive the reason for the elaborate framework of images and analogies by which he attempts to communicate to us the significance of time in the universe.

For what reason did the maker construct the universe (29d)? He was good, and no good being is envious; consequently he wanted to make the universe as good as pos-

[2] Cf. 53d, 59c-d, 68d, 72d.
[3] Cf., e.g., *Cratylus* 440c.

sible.[4] One rightly accepts the existence of this supreme
principle of becoming, says Timaeus, on the word of wise
men. (Taylor remarks that Timaeus "speaks the language
of religion rather than of 'scientific theology.'"[5] But of
course the religious basis is not essential to the argument. It
is intended to corroborate the dialectical maker we have set
up. We have already said that the universe is the fairest of
created things.) Wishing all good, and nothing evil as far as
possible, God (so the craftsman is called by Timaeus) took
over all that was visible, not at rest but moving without
harmony or order, and brought order out of disorder, deem-
ing that in every way better. It is not right for the best to
do other than the fairest. Among visible things nothing
without mind is fairer than a thing that possesses mind; but
mind cannot belong to anything apart from soul.[6] So he put
mind in soul and soul in body, in fashioning the universe, so
that he might be the creator of a work that was fairest and
best. Our probable account, says Timaeus, declares that the
universe is a living, rational animal through the providence
of God.

This probable account of Timaeus is fairly clear if we
perceive the metaphorical character of the argument. It is
not difficult to understand why the universe should be
thought of as a living animal; it seems to have a principle of
movement in itself as animals do, especially if we turn our
attention to the heavenly bodies, the revolution of the
heaven of fixed stars and the wanderings of the planets, all
of which Timaeus is to emphasize in his later account of
time. Why should the universe be said to possess mind? We
shall later note the regularity of motion in the universe, even

[4] We are told at *Phaedo* 97c–98b that things happen for the best;
everything is arranged as it is best for it to be. Cf. *Laws* 897c.
[5] *Op. cit.*, p. 78.
[6] Cf. *Sophist* 249a.

in those parts that would seem to the casual observer ir-regular. This regularity and order manifests rational pur-pose; but rational purpose can be due only to the presence in some way of mind in the universe.[7] But what are we to understand by the assertion of Timaeus that God brought order out of chaos? This is part of the same problem that we earlier postponed, but we need not enter into a detailed discussion for the moment. The passage tells us, however, that whatever order and harmony there is in the universe is due to the activity of intelligence, and without intelligence there is chaos. We see thus that the universe in becoming bears some trace of true being.

To what animal in the intelligible order was the universe made like, since it is an image of something else (30c)? It could be made like no incomplete animal, since that which is like the incomplete could not be fair. But it was likened to that animal of which the other intelligible animals are parts. We may call it the complete or perfect intelligible animal, since it embraces all intelligible animals just as the universe contains us and all other visible creatures. So God made the universe one, visible, containing all created animals within it. Timaeus then asks whether the universe is one or whether there are many or infinite universes. If constructed accord-ing to the model, he declares, it must be one. For there cannot be two model animals; if there were, there would have to be another embracing these two, and the universe would properly be likened to that third. Thus the universe in its solitude is like the perfect intelligible animal; there cannot be two or an infinite number.

Thus we learn that there can be only one perfect animal in the intelligible order, though many imperfect ones. Since there is but a single perfect animal as such, so the sensible

[7] Cf. *Philebus* 30a-c for this same point of view.

representation, in the account of Timaeus, must likewise be
one and all-embracing. Why cannot there be more than one
copy? Simply because all the imperfect animals in the intelligible order are included in the perfect animal. So there
can be no animal in the sensible order that is not included in
the complete scheme of the universe as a whole. There can
be nothing sensible, no matter how far it is removed from
everything else sensible, that is not a representation of something in the intelligible world; thus it is a part of the one
material universe. As Taylor puts it,

> there is thorough-going interconnexion between all the parts
> that make up 'nature'; whatever is 'sensible' at all stands in
> definite interconnexion with everything else that is sensible,
> and thus the complex of 'all the sensible' is a single system.[8]

Consequently, however many stellar systems we discover, it
will remain true that in one sense there is but a single universe, the parts of which are all connected with one another
by their reference to the intelligible order.

The fact that for the early cosmologists *ouranos* or *kosmos* [9] refers to a stellar or planetary system leads Taylor to
the remark, "It is in many ways unfortunate that Plato
should have confused the principle of the 'uniformity' of
nature with the assertion that there is only one 'stellar system.'" [10] But do we have any right to interpret the text as
saying that there is only one stellar system? Timaeus tells
us that there can be only one universe because the sensible
world is an imitation of the intelligible model.[11] From this
point of view we may say that the universe is one. But later
in the dialogue (55c-d) the question recurs. After saying

[8] *Op. cit.*, p. 85.
[9] They are used indifferently by Timaeus at 28b.
[10] *Op. cit.*, p. 85.
[11] Especially at 31a-b.

that the number of *kosmoi* is not infinite, Timaeus admits
that there might be difficulty in deciding whether there is
one or five (because of the five regular solids, apparently).
There is but one, he declares, from the standpoint of his own
likely story, but someone else from another point of view
might conjecture differently. This would seem to mean that
despite a possible multiplicity of *ouranoi* or *kosmoi* there is
still a sense in which there is but one. Taylor remarks on
the later passage, "Thus we may perhaps infer that Plato
admits that, but for considerations of the metaphysical
order, physics need not be committed to the hypothesis of
only one 'stellar system.' " [12] But the metaphysical order
imposes unity upon the physical order only in the way we
have mentioned; there is a sense in which we may say there
is but a single stellar system, though that complete system
may be composed of two or more parts each of which may
also receive the name of stellar system. Thus in modern
science the term "universe" may conceivably be applied to
a portion of the entire universe, so that one might speak of a
plurality of universes.[13] The relation between the sensible
and intelligible orders as set forth in the discussion determines in what sense we are to understand that there is a
single universe.

### THE BODY OF THE UNIVERSE

That the corporeal universe may be visible and tangible,
God compounds its body out of fire and earth (31b). These
are joined together, with air and water as middle terms, by
means of a proportion. For the best bond is that which
makes itself and the things joined one, and proportion is

---

[12] *Op. cit.*, p. 379.
[13] Aristotle is led to the doctrine of a single universe by an entirely
different analysis, *On the Heaven* 276a18–279a11.

best suited to do this.[14] On this compounding Taylor remarks,

> Of course this reasoning is not given by Plato as a *demonstration* that there must be neither more nor less than four 'roots'. It is simply a play of mathematical fancy, such as would naturally occur to a Pythagorean interested in bringing his arithmetic into connexion with the medicine of the Sicilian school originated by Empedocles.[15]

But we should not, of course, lose sight of the fact that we are told of mathematical laws at this point because order and harmony exist in the universe, and in the "mathematical fancy" we are to discern a serious purpose. We shall see later that order is thought of as arising chiefly from the soul of the universe; but there must be some basis likewise in the body. The unity brought about by this proportion emphasizes the indestructibility of the universe that is next mentioned. No part of any element, continues Timaeus, is left outside the body of the universe in order that it might be a complete whole from complete parts and that there might be nothing left from which another universe could be made. We thus reinforce our original assertion of the unity of the universe (from the standpoint of this likely story); there can, of course, be no such things as fire and earth apart from the whole material universe, because the universe is all the sensible world that exists. There is another reason offered by Timaeus, namely, in order that the universe might be ageless and healthy; for such things as heat and cold, attacking a compound body from without, waste it away. Timaeus is here taking an analogy from the bodies in our experience which suffer from an unfavorable environment. The material universe has no environment because

---

[14] Cf. *Gorgias* 508a.
[15] *Op. cit.*, p. 98.

there is nothing else. Timaeus has already told us that the body of the universe, being joined together by proportion, could not be destroyed except by the will of the maker (32c). So here he is repeating in a more concrete way that the universe is indestructible.[16]

Since the universe is to contain all animals, that figure which contains all figures was given to it (33b). The spherical figure is the most perfect and regular (the five regular solids, later used by Timaeus in the formation of the elements, can be inscribed in the sphere). As Taylor says,

The argument that the οὐρανός is spherical because all the regular polyhedra can be inscribed in the sphere is presumably to Plato himself, like a good many things in the dialogue, no more than a playful fancy but Timaeus may be meant to take it quite seriously.[17]

We have here, it is true, another likely story, but we should perceive the serious truth behind it that the universe must have that shape which is most appropriate to its nature. The universe, as Timaeus explains at some length, is self-sufficient, needing nothing else for its well-being (for there is nothing else). It is the only thing which acts upon itself, and it alone is affected by its own action. It came about thus from the art of the maker. It was given that motion most proper to it, the circular, and there was no other kind of motion present.

### THE SOUL OF THE UNIVERSE

The maker put a soul into the body, spreading it throughout and even enveloping the body from without (34b). So the universe, says Timaeus, moves in a circle, one and alone,

---

[16] For Aristotle too there is nothing outside of the heaven, *On the Heaven* 278b21–279a11, and it is indestructible, *ibid.* 281a27–284b5.

[17] *Op. cit.*, p. 101.

in its excellence needing nothing else, a happy god. Taylor refuses the interpretation of Proclus that the soul is said to envelop the body of the universe from without because it has a supramundane element in its constitution. He suggests that the statement is made "because Timaeus is thinking of the supposed diurnal revolution of the outermost heaven as the most uniform and orderly of all movements and thus as most fully revealing the presence of an intelligent ψυχή." [18] It is clear that the soul is spread throughout the universe to explain the motion and order to be observed everywhere in it; perhaps the soul is said to envelop the body even from without to emphasize the complete dominance of the intelligent harmony and purpose that pervade all things. But, continues Timaeus, we should not think that the soul was made later than the body; our mode of speaking about such things is a rather casual one. Rather the soul is the prior and the elder both in creation and in excellence.[19] The soul, according to this statement, need not have existed before the body of the universe so as to have been at any time without a body; all that is meant is that the soul is first in the order of nature, for the laws that operate in nature are in command of the materials in which they are embodied.

We come now to one of the most perplexing passages in the dialogue, the construction of the soul of the universe (35a). There has been a serious controversy on this point ever since the *Timaeus* began to be interpreted.[20] There are a few observations, most of them fairly clear, that are pertinent to the problem of time. The maker of the soul, says Timaeus, takes indivisible, unchanging being and being that becomes divisible in the realm of bodies. He prepares a

[18] *Op. cit.*, p. 105.
[19] Cf. *Laws* 895b.
[20] For a full discussion of this controversy see Taylor, *op. cit.*, pp. 109 ff.

mixture of these two and sets it in their midst. In the course of his description Timaeus seems to give the indivisible and divisible also the names of the Same and the Other. So the maker compounds the soul out of three elements. He first unites the Same and the Other by force, unwilling as they are to be joined together. Then he mixes them with the being that has already been formed by the combination of the indivisible and the divisible, or the Same and the Other. The mixture of these three elements makes a single soul.

This passage is illumined somewhat by a subsequent one (37a-c). Since the soul, says Timaeus, has been compounded from the Same, the Other, and the third being, whenever it meets with divided being or undivided being, it is able to pronounce identity and difference both in the realm of becoming and in that of changeless being. With regard to both identity and difference the soul possesses truth. In the realm of the sensible through the operation of the Other true opinions are formed; in the realm of the intelligible through the operation of the Same knowledge comes about. We have here and in other places an analogy between the soul of man and the soul of the universe thus constructed. Man is able to make judgments regarding identity and difference with reference to both intelligible and sensible objects; so we may think of the soul of man as compounded of the indivisible and the divisible, of the Same and the Other. Interpreted more literally we should say that like is known by like; so Aristotle ascribes this view to "Plato in the *Timaeus*." [21] Since we observe certain similarities between the actions of man and those of the universe, actions that show change and multiplicity but have a definite purpose guiding them in an orderly way, we may ascribe a soul to the universe that is analogous to that of man.

[21] *On the Soul* 404b16.

We should note the last sentence of this passage in the dialogue (37c): in whatever being these two things (opinion and knowledge) are present, if anyone says it is other than soul he will speak anything but the truth. The metaphor of soul is thus employed to account for the "truth of things," the basis of our knowledge of things.[22]

When the soul has been compounded, the maker marks off divisions in its substance according to a melodic progression (35b). Thus we see that the soul possesses harmony within itself, a harmony which it will communicate to the motion of the universe. The melodic progression goes far beyond that of the ordinary Greek musical scale or any musical scale, for, as Robin says, "la gamme que Platon a en vue n'est pas une gamme de fait, mais une gamme *de droit*." [23] The mixture of which the soul is compounded is all used up. Now the soul, having the form of a long band, with the divisions marked off, is cut lengthwise down the middle. These two halves are made to intersect in the middle, and are then bent so as to form two circles in different planes, touching each other at two diametrically opposed points. We are later told (39a) that one of the circles is tilted so that its plane is inclined obliquely to that of the other circle. For the two circles represent the sidereal or celestial equator (a projection of the earth's equator on the spherical heaven) and the ecliptic (the path made by the annual journey of the sun through the zodiac). We have been told (and shall be told again [36e]) that the soul is spread throughout the universe, for reasons already mentioned. In this place, however, through a new metaphor, the soul is represented as a kind of framework. It is easier to

[22] Timaeus later indicates (47b-c) that man learns to control the revolutions of reason within himself by observing the revolutions of reason in the heaven.

[23] Léon Robin, *Platon* (Paris: Alcan, 1938), p. 199.

represent the harmony in the soul of the universe by means of the two bands having the divisions marked off upon them. Moreover, the movement of the universe, which arises from the soul, is most visible in the motions of the sidereal equator and the ecliptic, which are next described.

Both of these circles are made to revolve, but in much different ways. One revolution is called that of the Same, the second that of the Other. The revolution of the sidereal equator accounts for the diurnal revolution of the fixed stars, a motion that appears very uniform. But the path of the sun and the planets through the ecliptic is to all appearances very irregular. We realize of course that both circles have the Same and the Other in their constitution; but the regular motion of one exemplifies better the identity of the universe with itself, the varied motion of the second the elements of difference in its constitution. The revolution of the Same is given sovereignty over that of the Other. For God allowed it to remain single and undivided, but the circle of the Other he split into seven unequal circles, seven concentric orbits answering partially to the musical progression already noted. We must keep in mind, as Taylor states,[24] that the Greeks thought of the orbit of the heavenly body as itself revolving and carrying the body with it, as a ring carries the stone that is set in it. So here, even before we hear of the bodies that are to revolve in their orbits, we find the orbits themselves in the soul of the universe. The order which exists in the motions of the heavenly bodies is an order that has its origin in the very soul of the *ouranos*. Again we realize the appropriateness of describing the soul in terms of the two circles. Of these seven orbits, three are completed in the same time, says Timaeus, but four differ from the other three and from one another, although the

[24] *Op. cit.*, p. 148.

speeds have a definite ratio. We should note here that the harmony originally put into the soul of the universe is not exhausted by giving rise to the motions of the various heavenly bodies; for the musical progression is more extensive than the number of orbits justifies.

Plutarch declares that there is harmony manifested in the body of the universe, leading back to an intelligent and good soul.[25] In general we may say that if there is going to be harmony and order in the universe there must be a more fundamental harmony in the soul of the universe, a harmony that is only partially, though in its most evident form, manifested in the motions of the heavenly bodies. The sovereignty of the circle of the Same has an astronomical significance, and in addition indicates that in spite of the diversity of the appearances there is a basic regularity in the motion of the universe. The maker joins together soul and body center to center (here we forget the circles), and the universe begins an endless life of reason. The body is visible; the soul is invisible and partakes of reason and harmony.

### THE CREATION OF TIME

When God saw the universe moving and living he was glad and tried to make it still more like the model (37c). Since the model is an everlasting animal, he tried to make the universe the same as far as it was possible. But the nature of animal as such is eternal, and to give this nature altogether to something created was not possible. So he thought to make a moving image of eternity, and in the very act of ordering the universe he made an image of eternity abiding as it is in unity, an eternal image proceeding according to number. This image we call time. Days, nights, months, and years did not exist before the creation of the universe,

[25] *De Animae Procreatione in Timaeo* 1029d.

but came into being when it was fashioned. All these are parts of time, and "was" and "will be" are created forms of time. We wrongly apply such terms to the eternal being; of it we should say only "is," never "was" or "will be." "Was" and "will be" belong to becoming that proceeds in time, for they are motions. The eternal being does not become older or younger because of time, nor do any of the processes that becoming attaches to sensible objects pertain to the eternal being; all these have come to be as forms of time. Time imitates eternity and goes around according to number. Time was created along with the universe, so that being produced together they might perish together if ever there should be any perishing; and according to the model of the eternal nature, so that it might be as like as possible to that model. The model is through all eternity; time has come into being, is and will be continuously throughout all time.

From the providence of God, therefore, that time might be created, the sun, moon, and planets were created to distinguish and guard the numbers of time. Making their bodies, God put them into the orbits, seven in number, made by the revolution of the circle of the Other. They were then assigned their duties, to assist in the fashioning of time. In order that there might be some clear measure of the relative speed and slowness with which these beings completed their orbits, God put a light in the second orbit from the earth, which we call the sun, that it might shine to the farthest reaches of heaven, and that all animals to whom it is fitting might partake of number, learning it from the uniform revolution of the Same. There is a month when the moon overtakes the sun, a year when the sun completes its orbit. Few men note the revolutions of the others, or name them, or measure them against one another by means of numbers; that is to say, they do not know that time is the wanderings of these bodies, many and intricate as they are. The perfect number of time fills the perfect year when all the orbits resume their starting position. Thus the planets were created in order that the universe might be as like as possible to the perfect intelligible animal, by imitation of the eternal nature.

This treatment of time shows us first of all that time and the universe are inseparable, and that time came into being with the ordering of the universe. We should look upon time as somehow resulting from the activity of mind in the created order; for time does not belong to that which is not created. Timaeus insists throughout that time is something that makes the universe more like its model than it would be without time; this cannot be, of course, for the reason that time involves change, because that is the chief difference between the eternal being and anything produced. Change is something that necessarily belongs to becoming. But time is an aspect of that change that bridges the gap, as it were, between change and the immutability of the eternal nature. Thus time, as Timaeus conceives it, does not belong to becoming as such (he will emphasize this point later) but to becoming that has been set in order by mind in accordance with an eternal model. Time is a moving image; insofar as it is moving it is unlike eternity. But it is made an image by being set in motion in a certain way by the ordering power of mind. Just as the universe is thought of as distinct from the chaos contrasted with it, so time is different from whatever duration that chaos may possess.

Eternity in its immutability is said to abide in unity. This is of course impossible for time, since the universe is created and subject to change and diversity. But this diversity can be assimilated to immutability if it is made to proceed in a measured way, according to number. Number is contrasted with unity insofar as anything that is numbered embodies diversity; but the regular progression of a numerical series bears a resemblance to unity, is a kind of projection of unity.[26] It applies to a diversity in which a rational principle is present as a source of regularity and order. It is this ordered regularity of time that makes it an imitation of eternity; moreover, time and the universe persist throughout all time just as the eternal nature endures through all eternity.

### THE "INSTRUMENTS OF TIME"

We now come to the important function of the sun, moon, and planets in the creation of time (38c). These, according to Timaeus, were fashioned to distinguish and guard the numbers of time in order that time might be created. He seems to say that the creation of time after the eternal model involved the distinguishing and guarding of the numbers of time. Time is an image proceeding according to number and consequently must have numbers, that is, must be numerable or measurable. This measurability takes two different forms in the universe, the two circles of the Same and the Other. The motion of the Same is uniform and regular; it is in a certain sense representative of the self-identity of the universe. But the motion of the Other is broken up into seven subordinate motions; this expresses the diversity present in the universe as a consequence of its being in the order of becoming. We should not lose sight of the fact that these seven motions are really conceived as being in their totality the revolution of the circle of the Other.[27]

Thus Timaeus perceives in the wanderings of the sun,

[26] For the Pythagorean treatment of this, cf. Taylor, *op. cit.*, p. 187.

[27] Cf. 36c, where the maker is said to make the circles of the Same and the Other revolve with a circular motion, and 38c, where the seven orbits are said to be made by the revolution of the Other.

moon, and planets a diversity typical of the diversity of the
universe, but this diversity is somehow under the influence
of the circle of the Same.[28] Time is thought of especially
with reference to the circle of the Other, that is, the seven
orbits just mentioned. The regular procession of time according to number manifests itself in the seven different
orbits of the Other; these are of course governed by the
circle of the Same, but it is their diversity that gives time its
measurability. They provide the numbers according to
which time proceeds. Their wanderings by their diversity
distinguish the numbers, but by their fundamental regularity
they guard the numbers as well. In this way time is said to
be created by the very distinguishing and guarding of the
numbers. We might admit the possibility that time could
be created by other numbers than the ones actually present
in the universe; but Timaeus gives no explanation of the
necessity for the present system.

A great deal of light is thrown upon this view of time by
the additional declaration of Timaeus that time *is* the wanderings of the sun, moon, and planets. Time is a moving
image and the motion of these bodies along with the motion
of the sidereal equator is thought of as being the most fundamental motion in the universe. For we have seen that the
soul of the universe, from which all its activity arises, manifests itself most prominently in the two great circles. So it
is fitting that time should be identified with the motions that
make the universe itself a moving image of the eternal nature (though Timaeus does not use this expression explicitly), especially in view of the fact that these motions provide the numbers by virtue of which time has a regular
procession. The planets are also spoken of as the beings that
were to assist in the fashioning of time. Time is created

[28] Cf. 38e–39b.

primarily by the maker of the universe in the very act of ordering the universe in accordance with the eternal model and producing the moving image of eternity. But time could not be created unless there were something to proceed according to number in the realm of becoming. This procession according to number, as we have seen, is effected by the sun, moon, and planets. In two subsequent passages (41e and 42d) the sun, moon, and planets are referred to as "instruments of times" (ὄργανα χρόνων) and "instruments of time" (ὄργανα χρόνου). The fact that they assist in the fashioning of time makes the term ὄργανα very appropriate; they are the instruments by which the maker fashions the moving image of eternity, though it is still true that the wanderings of these bodies are, in their totality, the moving image itself.

The difference between χρόνων and χρόνου, the plural and singular, is noteworthy. The diversity by which the image of eternity manifests itself as moving is time, but each of those diverse aspects may itself be called a time. The motion of the universe appears most clearly in the two circles, especially, for the purposes of our exposition, in the circle of the Other, which is the collective name for the motions of the sun, moon, and planets. Taken thus collectively they form a single time, which is the image proceeding in accordance with the numbers they provide. But the motion of each of these bodies, taken in relation to the other motions, is in a limited way an image proceeding according to number, though the numbers in any individual case are less complex than those of time as a whole. So time is made up of individual times, and the perfect number of time is fulfilled when the complex numbers of all the individual times assume the relation to one another that they had at the beginning.

## ARISTOTELIAN INTERPRETATIONS OF PLATO

Later writers give as Plato's definition of time "the revolution of the universe" or something of the sort.[29] But others, probably influenced by the Aristotelian definition of time, consider time to be the measure of motion.[30] This sort of definition introduces the Aristotelian concept of time, a procedure that was not unusual in the later tradition and has not been restricted to the ancient Greeks. Xenocrates defines time as "the measure of created things and eternal motion," [31] a kind of mixture. The Aristotelian definition of time has likewise had a profound influence upon modern scholars. Though Taylor says, "It seems to me . . . that the *language* of Timaeus plainly *identifies* time with the uniform motion of a planet," [32] he nevertheless feels obliged to read into the thought of Timaeus something that the language does not justify. In his appendix on "The Concept of Time in the *Timaeus*," he declares that

χρόνος is not the same thing as the fundamental 'passage' of nature, the fact that nature is 'what goes on'. The name for this passage in Plato and Aristotle is κίνησις. . . . Time, according to both Plato and Aristotle, is not the 'passage' itself, but the 'measure' (μέτρον) or 'number' (ἀριθμός) of κίνησις.[33]

A similar view is held by Burnet, who says, "We can only think of motion as in time, for time is just the measure of motion." [34] But, as Taylor agrees, the language of Timaeus

---

[29] Theophrastus *Physicae Opiniones* Fr. 15 (Diels, *Doxographi Graeci* [Berlin: Reimer, 1879], p. 492); Aetius *Placita* i. 22 (Diels, *op. cit.*, p. 318); Aristotle quite possibly has Plato in mind, *Physics* 218a33–b1, 223b21–22.

[30] So [Plato] *Definitiones* 411b, "Time is the motion of the sun, the measure of locomotion."

[31] Ap. Aetius *op. cit.* i. 22 (p. 318).

[32] *Op. cit.*, p. 191.

[33] *Ibid.*, p. 680.

[34] John Burnet, *Greek Philosophy, Part I, Thales to Plato* (London: Macmillan, 1914), p. 342.

identifies time with the motion of the universe. How then are we justified in reading into Plato the Aristotelian definition of time, which, as we shall see, was formulated on the basis of an altogether different analysis?

It is possible for men to receive a notion of time from observing the heavenly bodies and thus provide themselves with a measure of motion. So Timaeus declares that the sun is made a radiant body in order that there may be a clear measure of the relative speeds of the planets, and in order that men may partake of number by watching the regular recurrence of day and night (39b-c). But men, he continues, do not realize that time *is* the wanderings of all seven bodies, nor do they measure them against one another by means of numbers. Taylor's presupposition that Plato and Aristotle have the same definition of time leads him to remark on this last sentence,

> This is because they think of the path of a planet as a mere πλάνη, an irregular 'stroll' or 'ramble'. Hence they do not understand that it is really 'time', i.e. that you could measure the passage of events just as well by the regular revolutions of any other body as by those of the sun or moon. The period of Mars is just as much a 'natural unit' for estimating duration as what we call a month or a year.[35]

This statement is in a sense true. If the revolution of any planet is time, then we can measure a passage of events by means of it, provided we recognize the true situation. But the point is that our measuring passage by means of the planet's revolution does not make that revolution time. The fact that we measure anything by means of time, that is, the motion of the planets, is only incidental to the real nature of time, which is to be a moving image of eternity. Timaeus has just told us that from observing the heavens we receive

[35] *Op. cit.*, p. 215.

our idea of number. He says later (47a-b), in telling of the real cause of vision in men, that the sight of night, day, months, and years has fashioned number and the notion of time, and has given men the study of the universe, from all of which philosophy has been derived. Thus men partake of number because there is number in the motions of the heavenly bodies above them. Timaeus also says that men receive their idea of time from the heavenly bodies. Equipped with these two things man is in a position to measure motion by numbers and by time. But the narrator insists that he receives these things from a universe in which they already exist. Man's knowledge is incidental to the nature of number and time in the universe outside of him. These things are present in the universe because it is an imitation of the eternal nature fashioned by a mind, a mind that strives to bring about a perfection of the image similar as far as it can be to that of the model. Taylor is surely nearer to the correct interpretation when he states,

The visible οὐρανός has its life in time, not in eternity, but the way in which its life is made up of unending cycles of motion is the nearest approach which 'passage' (τὸ γιγνόμενον) can make to the abiding self-sameness and quiet of eternity. It is this recurrence of the same great cosmical rhythm (the unit of the rhythm, the 'bar' of the music, so to say, being the τέλεος ἐνιαυτός), that Timaeus had in his mind when he called time a 'moving image of eternity'.[36]

But his observations as a whole are damaged by the unwarranted supposition that for Plato as well as for Aristotle time is the measure of motion.

Taylor, as quoted above, declares that Plato distinguishes between time and the passage of nature, χρόνος and κίνησις. But Timaeus, if we are to look at his language, says (37e-

[36] *Ibid.*, p. 221.

38a) that "was" and "will be" are created forms of time that we should not refer to the eternal nature. "Was" and "will be" should properly be spoken only with regard to becoming that proceeds in time, for they are motions (κινήσεις). Moreover, no processes, such as growing old, that becoming attaches to the objects of perception belong to the eternal, immutable nature; these are forms of time that have come into being. The context indicates that these motions and processes, as we observe them in the universe, are not pure becoming, but rather the becoming of a universe that has been ordered, that is, time.

It is not, therefore, surprising that Taylor should interpret other statements of Timaeus as he does. Thus the sun, moon, and planets " 'divide' or 'determine' the numbers, because we use their revolutions as units for measuring time; they 'guard' the numbers, keep them safe, in fact provide a *standard* measure, in virtue of the equability of the revolutions." [37] Again Taylor has fastened upon an incidental feature of time and its numbers, not its essential characteristic for Timaeus. At 38a time is said to imitate eternity and circle according to number. This would seem to be a clear indication that time is to be closely identified with the motion of the universe. Far from stating that time is the measure of motion, Timaeus rather tends to say that motion, that is, the motion of the universe, is the measure of time, for the heavenly bodies provide the numbers of time. But, as we have seen, though this is in a sense true, it is also true to say that these very motions are nothing different from time. The final sentence in the section devoted to time has a significance that Taylor notes but forgets in his general interpretation. Timaeus declares (39d-e) that the sun, moon, and planets were created in order that the universe might

[37] *Ibid.*, p. 192.

be made as like as possible to the perfect intelligible animal
by imitation of the eternal nature. But the universe is thus
assimilated to the eternal nature by time created as an image
of eternity. This would have no significance if time were
only something to be used by men as a measure. The essential function of time is to be an image and thereby make the
universe a more perfect imitation of the perfect nature that
abides in eternity. But the wanderings of the planets are
identified with time. We are told that time is a means of
making the universe more like the eternal nature and again
that the planetary bodies have the same function. This
should make it clear without dispute that Plato is not fundamentally in agreement with Aristotle on the definition of
time.

### RATIONAL AND SUBSIDIARY CAUSES IN THE UNIVERSE

There are some subsequent matters in the dialogue that
are pertinent to the problem of time. Timaeus proceeds
(39e) with the creation of the stars, which are thought of as
gods, possessed of a more regular motion than the planetary
bodies. Then comes the creation of man. His mortal part
is given to the gods to form. His soul, however, is fashioned
by God in the same way as the soul of the universe and from
the same elements, though inferior in quality. The souls are
then assigned each to a star, whence they view the universe
and learn its laws. They are told that they are to be sown in
the various planets and come to birth in mortal bodies. To
lead a good life they will have to overcome the senseless
matter about them, following the circle of the Same in a
well-regulated existence. Timaeus is implying here a close
connection between the study of the universe, philosophy,
and the moral life within the soul of man. By observing the
universe and seeing the purpose involved in it the soul can

establish a definite rule of conduct so as to govern the body with all its desires. That principle within the soul by which it retains its identity amid the changing world of matter and establishes itself as mistress of the body is called the circle of the Same, analogous to the circle of the Same in the soul of the universe.

As Timaeus continues his account we see that the circles of the soul are in conflict with the body when the soul and body are first joined together. Since neither is entirely the master, the entire being is moved about without order or rule. So Timaeus describes the mental confusion of the infant whose soul has not yet asserted itself as rational. The soul is attacked by sensations that shake the circles; they arrest the motion of the Same altogether and prevent it from ruling, or indeed proceeding at all, and they twist the circle of the Other out of shape. Timaeus explains this statement partially by saying that the soul is then wrong in judgments about identity and difference, because the circles are not ruling or guiding. But as time goes on the circles begin to settle down, and the process is made complete by a correct education.

After a discussion of the structure of the eye Timaeus points out (46c) that the physical principles he has just laid down with regard to the process of seeing are only the subordinate causes which God uses in achieving the best.[38] Most scientists think that heating, cooling, and other such things are causes in their own right. But they cannot be other than the subsidiary causes that mind uses; for mind belongs to soul alone, and soul is invisible. The lover of wisdom should seek first for causes in the rational order, later for those that are subsidiary. There are then two kinds of causes, says Timaeus, those that produce good and fair

[38] Cf. *Phaedo* 96a–99d.

effects through the operation of mind, and those lacking
rational power that produce effects without direction or
order. As Taylor remarks,[39] we need not think that any
such agent is working independently in the universe; but if
such a mechanism were acting in an undirected way, it
would produce effects without reference to any good. Having considered the subsidiary causes of sight, declares Timaeus, we can now give the real cause. From seeing the
heavenly bodies and their motions men have received the
idea of number and of time, and in general the study of
nature. As a result of these activities man has obtained philosophy, the greatest gift of the gods. The revolutions in
the heavens should provide a model for the revolutions of
thought, which are related to them, as the troubled to the
serene. Learning the revolutions in the heavens, computing
their ratios, and imitating their unerring movements, we
should guide aright the straying movements within us. Thus
Timaeus again affirms the relation between the laws of
science and the rules of ethics and the good moral life.[40] We
should be interested to note that man receives the notion of
time as well as the knowledge of number from his observations of the heavenly bodies. Both of these exist in the
universe as part of the divine plan; when we find them we
have caught a glimpse of the real cause of the universe, not
causes and processes that are merely subsidiary. As Timaeus
had put it previously,[41] the various beings within the universe exist for the sake of making it complete. But now we
see that in a sense the universe exists for man. It is by observing the universe and the laws embodied in it that man is
enabled to lead a good life, and among the contributions

[39] *Op. cit.*, p. 293.
[40] He repeats these ideas at later points in the dialogue; cf. 88c–89a,
90d, 91e.
[41] 39e–40a.

made by the heavens to man is the notion of time. There is nothing in the narrative to indicate that time in its essential nature is other than the motion of the divinely ordered universe.

So far, continues Timaeus (47e), we have been talking for the most part about the things that were fashioned by mind; now we should add those things that came to be through necessity. For the creation of the universe was a mixture of these two things. Mind persuaded necessity to bring most created things to the best end, and if we wish to give a complete account of the universe we must add an account of the errant cause, necessity. We must now examine what came before the creation of the universe, what were the natures of fire, air, water, and earth. Our previous exposition of the universe distinguished between the model, intelligible and unchanging, and the imitation, created and visible. But now a third thing is perceived to be made necessary by the demands of our dialectical discourse, a receptacle and nurse, as it were, of all becoming. Just as the gold which is being moulded into various shapes is that in which the shapes appear, so this receptacle has always the function of receiving all things. It is that in which all things come to be and perish. Even the four elements are not permanent; we see them constantly changing into one another. But our receptacle as receptacle is permanent. It is moved and shaped by the various things that enter it; these things that come and go are imitations of unchanging beings. So we now have to distinguish three things in our discourse, that which becomes, that in which it becomes, and that which is imitated by the thing that becomes. There is being, unchanging, unproduced, indestructible, admitting nothing else and entering into no other, imperceptible and grasped only by thought. That which imitates it and is called after it is produced, perceptible, coming to be in a certain place and perishing there, grasped by opinion along with sensation. The receptacle is space, admitting no destruction, providing a place for all things that become, grasped not by perception but by a kind of bastard reasoning that can hardly be called belief. The true being is not in space, but the image, since it was fashioned after another, fittingly comes to be in another, thus barely partaking of being.

So there were being, space, and becoming even before the creation of the universe. Space was filled with the random, lawless movements of the four elements. The irregular motion of the receptacle whirls about the contents like a sieve; particles of like character tend to be assembled together, while the unlike are separated. So these things took different places even before the universe was fashioned from them. Before this all of them were without ratio or measure. When the universe was ordered the elements, having certain traces of what they are now, but arranged as anything is when God is absent from it, were then first ordered by God with forms and numbers (the geometrical forms and numerical formulas are given by Timaeus later). God put together these things, so far as possible, as the fairest and the best, though they were not so before.

The narrative concerned with the role of necessity in the creation of the universe has brought about a great deal of controversy, most of which is not pertinent here. It seems clear that necessity is nothing different from the subsidiary causes previously mentioned by Timaeus.[42] But the reason for calling this cause necessity is not immediately clear. Some think that it is mechanical causality.[43] Martin thinks

[42] Cf. later passages in the dialogue, especially 56c and 68e–69b.
[43] So Robin, *op. cit.*, pp. 221 f., 235.

of necessary ontological laws; "la nécessité est une puissance aveugle, qui après avoir régné seule sur la matière éternelle, est obligée, sans abdiquer, de se soumettre à l'action supérieure de la Providence, qui vient enfin organiser le monde." [44] Baeumker asks how necessity can be mechanical causality if it is said to be persuaded by mind.[45] (This objection seems to lack force. Fire can be thought of as burning necessarily by mechanical causality; but since it is purely mechanical it does so without reference to any good end. It can be "persuaded" by mind to effect a good end. Thus fire can be made to heat the house instead of burning it down, though fire in itself is indifferent to either of these ends.) He declares that the subsidiary causes are called necessary because they are the indispensable instruments that mind must have to effect its purpose.[46] What happens through necessity is

die Summe der Momente in der körperlichen Natur, welche nicht aus ihrer durch den göttlichen Weltbildner bewirkten Durchseelung vermittelst der Weltseele resultieren, sondern welche jene notwendig vorauszusetzende körperliche Natur entweder schon beim Beginn der Weltordnung mitbrachte, oder welche sie doch selbst, freilich unter der "Überredung", d. h. Leitung der Vernunft, hervorbringen kann.[47]

Another view is put forward by Taylor.[48]

But, whatever is the precise reason for the term, there are some very important observations we may make with regard to time on the basis of Timaeus' discourse on necessity. We see what Timaeus referred to when he said previously

---

[44] T. H. Martin, *Études sur le Timée de Platon* (Paris: Ladrange, 1841), II, 171 f.

[45] C. Baeumker, *Das Problem der Materie in der griechischen Philosophie* (Münster: Aschendorff, 1890), p. 118.

[46] *Ibid.*, pp. 119 ff.

[47] *Ibid.*, p. 124.

[48] *Op. cit.*, pp. 300 f.

that the maker of the universe took the visible, disorderly mass and reduced it to order. Before the creation of the ordered universe the elements were without any arrangement; not only did they exist independently of any *kosmos* but even in themselves there was no harmony (52d). They had only a vague likeness to what they became when they were given a stable order by God and made to constitute a rational, coherent universe. In them there was an attraction of like for like, but the elements did not have any regular motions because there were no definite structures in their bodies. This was remedied, according to the later account of Timaeus (53c), when God chose the fairest triangles to constitute the elements. Thus mind is responsible for all the order in the universe, not only the arrangement of the whole out of the elements, but the inward harmony of the elements themselves as well.

### THE RELATION OF TIME, SPACE, AND MOTION

The question now arises whether we should accept the account of Timaeus to mean that a chaos really existed before the creation of the ordered universe, so that the universe would have a beginning. This was the interpretation of Aristotle, who criticizes Plato for saying that the universe, though generated, will always be,[49] that the ordered arose out of the unordered,[50] and that both time and the universe had a beginning.[51] But most of the Academics, from Xenocrates onward, explain that Plato does not mean to say that there was a beginning of time and of the universe. According to Xenocrates, when Plato speaks of time and the universe as beginning he does so merely for the sake

[49] *On the Heaven* 280a30–32.
[50] *Ibid.* 300b17–18.
[51] *Physics* 251b17–19. It is characteristic of Aristotle's method to criticize his predecessors on the basis of a literal interpretation.

of exposition, just as geometers speak of drawing a line or constructing a square, though they cannot make a real geometrical line or figure.[52] The Neo-Platonists held in general that the universe is not generated in the sense that it had a beginning of time, but is generated insofar as it is a product and is dependent upon something other than itself. But Plutarch in his own fashion accepts the account of Timaeus literally.[53] It is perhaps impossible to decide with finality what Plato really held on this point, and it is not essential to his treatment of time — as it is considered here — to pursue the matter in greater detail.[54]

But whether the distinction between chaos and the ordered universe is merely logical or indicates some kind of chronological priority, there are certain consequences that inevitably follow for the Platonic concept of time. Taylor may be correct in his interpretation of Plato when he accepts the logical distinction, remarking, "Apart from the activity of God, if *per impossibile* you could 'eliminate God' from the scheme of things, law and order would vanish, you would be left with mere chaotic confusion." [55] But many of his statements directed against the chronological priority are vitiated by his unwarranted assumption with regard to Plato's definition of time. He says, "No sane man could be meant to be understood literally in maintaining at once that time and the world began together, and also that there was a state of things . . . . *before* there was any world." [56] Again, the creation of time "is not to be taken literally, since

---

[52] For a criticism of this view see Aristotle *On the Heaven* 279b32–280a10.

[53] *Op. cit.* 1016c-f.

[54] Cf. Robin, *op. cit.*, p. 229, "L'état antérieur à l'existence du monde doit donc être, logiquement ou chronologiquement peu importe, un état de mobilité universelle, incessante et sans règle, un état d'absolu désordre."

[55] *Op. cit.*, p. 80.

[56] *Ibid.*, p. 69.

it would then imply the absurd consequence that there 'was
a time' when as yet there was no time." [57]  Finally,

> When Timaeus says that ὄν and γένεσις and χώρα were there
> 'even before the birth of the οὐρανός' . . . . his words are not
> to be taken literally. All through his discourse οὐρανός and τὸ
> γενόμενον have been treated as synonymous; nature is just
> what 'passes', γίγνεται, and there would be no sense in talking
> about a 'passage', γένεσις, which was there before there was any
> nature. We cannot even, with Plutarch, take him to mean that
> there once was purely random and chaotic 'passage' as opposed
> to 'passage' which exhibits law and order, since he has told us
> that 'time came to be *along with* (ἅμα) the οὐρανός.' [58]

Taking the chaos as distinct from the universe in a logical
sense, Taylor says that if there could be any motion without
the directing power of mind this motion would be disorderly
and confused. That is to say, order and harmony are the
work of mind. But Timaeus is just as emphatic in saying
that time is due to the activity of mind in the universe,
fashioning a moving image of eternity. Without mind, just
as there would not be order, so there would not be time.
Timaeus is saying that order and time belong to a certain
scheme of things; motion as such does not belong there.
Taylor's difficulty again is his application of the Aristotelian
definition of time. If time is the measure of motion, then, of
course, the moving chaos will have to exist in time. Then if
time is created simultaneously with a universe that arises out
of an actually existing chaos, Plato would be saying that
time is created after time exists. This is the absurdity that
Taylor wishes to avoid. But even if the chaos did not really
exist before the universe we are still in difficulty with
Taylor's interpretation. Let us suppose that there is not a
temporal but only a logical distinction between the chaos

[57] *Ibid.*, p. 184.
[58] *Ibid.*, p. 352.

and the universe. But time, as well as order, belongs to the universe and not to that which is so pointedly distinguished from the universe by Timaeus. Then if time is present to the chaotic matter, time is logically distinct from time. But that would seem to be a conclusion that is equally absurd as that which says that time has a chronological priority to time. The Aristotelian concept of time must surely, therefore, be kept out of the *Timaeus*.

We can say, if we wish, that the chaos, being in motion, had a duration or persistence that involved change. This is the sort of duration that Aristotle and Taylor would call time. But for Timaeus it is not time; that which men have called time is a moving image of eternity, an image that proceeds according to number. It is something fashioned by the mind of God and exists, logically and chronologically, along with an ordered universe. Moreover, even if the οὐρανός and τὸ γενόμενον are treated as synonymous at certain places in the narrative, that is because the universe is the production with which we are here concerned. When Timaeus says that being, becoming, and space were before the creation of the universe, he is distinguishing these things from the universe, if not literally in a chronological sense, then in some logical sense. The universe is not synonymous with "what becomes," for it involves much more in its constitution than becoming; so time does not belong to becoming as such, since becoming was before the universe, but only to the peculiar kind of "what becomes" this universe is.

There is one further difficulty to be disposed of. Timaeus states (52c) that, since all coming to be is only an image of real being, it is fitting that, as the image of something other than itself, that which comes to be should exist in something other than itself, that is, in space. In this way it clings to existence as best it can and escapes utter not-being. A spatial order thus somehow exists through the exigencies of coming to be. This leads Taylor to remark that Timaeus seems to suggest that *"because the* γιγνόμενον *is 'in time' it is also 'in space'; occupation of space is, in some way, a consequence of occupation of time."* [59] This statement is in a sense true, but it is not completely accurate unless we accept the Aristotelian for the Platonic time. That which comes to be must have a duration that is connected with change, but this alone does not make time for Plato. This kind of duration, which Timaeus does not mention explicitly, requires existence in space. But to exist in time is something more than to have a duration that involves change. It is correct to say that the temporal order involves the spatial order, but this places a wrong emphasis on the doctrine set forth by Timaeus. Even before the creation of time there is space. Even the elements have some resemblance to their true selves before the creation of the universe (53b), although there is no proportion in them except that which results from chance (69b). Thus the elements can exist after a fashion in a spatial order that is not temporal as well. The temporal order for Plato involves the spatial, not insofar as it is temporal, but insofar as time is a kind of duration that involves change. The order and regularity that are necessarily present in time are over and above the realm of changing spatial things.

The misplaced emphasis in this last view of Taylor leads to the error to be noted also in the statement of Burnet, who says, "besides being temporal, the 'errant cause' is spatial." [60] But the dialogue very clearly includes time among the things which are the product of mind, not of necessity. At 47e Timaeus retraces his steps to narrate the role of necessity

[59] *Ibid.*, p. 349.
[60] *Op. cit.*, p. 343.

in the creation of the universe. Long before that he had described the creation of time by God. A duration that involves change, as was said above, must be in space. But time brings into this duration a regularity that assimilates the realm of becoming to that of unchanging being. Being and becoming are somehow linked together when the latter is made temporal, for it is the resemblance between time and eternity that Timaeus insists upon rather than their difference. The "errant cause," therefore, is not temporal in the Platonic sense. It is the universe that is temporal because in the creation of the universe mind is at work likening the imitation that has come into being as much as possible to the model that is unchanging.

# ARISTOTLE

## *Time, the Number of Motion*

THE Aristotelian discussion of time is for the most part limited to the *Physics*, which has as its subject matter nature and problems connected with nature. So in the science of nature the first task is to attempt to determine what relates to the principles (184a14–16). In the first book Aristotle takes up the principles proposed by others, showing how they are inadequate as an explanation of nature, although they lead in the right direction. Then he proposes his own theory of matter, form, and privation as the principles of nature and especially of the change which occurs in nature. At the end of this book (192b2–3) Aristotle declares that he has established that there are principles and has discussed their nature and number. The book closes with the statement that we are to make a fresh start and proceed on the study of nature.

### THE SUBJECT MATTER OF NATURAL PHILOSOPHY

The second book begins without any explicit reference to the subject matter of the first; it consists of an analysis of nature, the principles of which we have already studied. Nature is defined (192b20–22) as a principle and cause of motion and rest in that to which they belong primarily. The four causes are introduced in the third chapter of the second book. Since the causes are four, it is the business of the student of nature to know about all of them, and he will give a proper account of nature by referring his problems to them, the matter, form, mover, and end (198a22–24). In the third book, since nature is a principle of motion and change (200b12–13), we find that we must go seriously into the nature of motion and then into related matters. We thus lay down a method of procedure that carries us through the third and fourth books. The infinite, place, void, and time all seem to be involved in motion. These things are thought to be attributes common to all the objects in the science of nature and they should consequently be studied before any special attributes that are not common. Motion is defined (201a10–11) as the actualization of the potential insofar as it is potential. So when that which can be built, insofar as it is just that, is being actualized, it is being built, and this is the process or motion of building. Now motion is supposed to be continuous. The infinite presents itself in the continuous, for the continuous is found to be infinitely divisible. Aristotle proves that there can be no actual infinite body. The infinite is a potential existence, but such a potential that it can never exist in actuality. Magnitude is divisible infinitely; that is, it can always continue to be divided. Number may be increased infinitely; that is, we can always add to it. But there cannot be an actually existing infinite magnitude or number. In the fourth book Aristotle discusses place. Then he takes up the void, and denies that it exists. Previous thinkers had used the void to explain motion, but motion, Aristotle thinks, can be explained without the void, and, moreover, the existence of the void is impossible. Finally we come to the last of the subjects proposed at the beginning of the third book, time.

The treatment of time extends from the tenth to the fourteenth chapter of the fourth book. It is important for the Aristotelian analysis to follow the argument in the order laid down by Aristotle. Much of the misunderstanding of the passage has arisen from abandoning the order of treatment followed by Aristotle and from supposing that certain statements about time in other contexts are to be understood in the present argument. This is to impress a mode of procedure upon Aristotle that disregards the order of the work that has come down to us, a method that introduces elements into a context that are improper and foreign to it, if there is to be admitted the rigorous procedure that he seems in general to follow.

We shall note that the Aristotelian definition of time is due in large measure to the mode of analysis he employs. He does not begin with the broad world-view that we have seen employed in the *Timaeus*, into which time enters as an essential ingredient in the universe as a whole, an ingredient which cannot be understood without reference to that universe and indeed to all reality, within the universe and outside of it. At a certain stage in the Aristotelian argument the universe will enter the picture and will be seen to have a connection with time that is reminiscent of the Platonic world-view. But the analysis of time in this section of the *Physics* presupposes nothing about the universe. As we have seen, Aristotle is interested in a search for the principles and causes of nature and of the attributes considered common to nature as a whole. But nature is a principle of motion and change, and motion is thought to involve time. Thus time lies within the scope of the student of nature. He is to see if there is any justification in the view that motion and time are related; if they are related, it is his task to determine the exact relation. Thus time is considered as a term to be analyzed within the rather narrow framework of nature, and more specifically of motion. It is studied with reference to the motion that is presented to the natural philosopher when he considers the world about him. There is no concern with the production of a universe that will contain motion and time. Motion and time already exist. How will the student of nature analyze them?

### DIFFICULTIES CONCERNING TIME

To begin his investigation Aristotle takes up (217b30) difficulties about time that have arisen in general discussions. First of all, does time exist or not? There are certain considerations that would make one suspect that it does not exist at all or at best in a rather obscure way. For part of it has gone and is no longer, part is still to come and is not yet. Indefinite time or any limited section, such as a year or a day, consists of these two parts. But a thing which is composed of nonexistent parts can hardly seem to deserve the name of existent. In the second place (considering time as divisible rather than composite), if any divisible thing is going to exist, it would seem that all or some of its parts must then exist. But of time some parts have gone, some are to come; not one actually exists, though time is divisible. We should not think of the moment or now as a part, for a part measures the whole and the whole is compounded of its parts. But time does not seem to be compounded of nows.[1] A third difficulty concerns the now itself; it is not easy to see whether the now, which appears to divide the past and the future, is always the same or different. If the now is always different, then an earlier now must have ceased to be

---

[1] This denial is taken up explicitly later, *Physics* 231b6–10.

by the present time. But the now could not have ceased to be in itself, for that was just when it existed. Nor could it have ceased to exist in another now. For we must say that nows cannot be next to one another, any more than points.[2] If the now ceased to be in some other now than itself, it would also exist in the intermediate nows (which are infinite in number, just as between any two points on a line there are infinite points) simultaneously with them, which is impossible. If the now cannot always be different, yet it cannot always be the same. For no divisible finite thing has but a single limit. But we can take a limited time, which would not be possible if the now which is the end of the time is the same as that which was the beginning. Moreover, if to be simultaneous is to be in the same now, then no event will be earlier or later than any other. For all will be in the same now, and the events of ten thousand years ago will be simultaneous with those of today.

Thus we may dismiss the attributes of time and pass on to its nature. But this has been left just as obscure by traditional views as by our preliminary considerations. Some say it is the movement of the universe (possibly a reference to Plato), others the sphere itself. Time cannot be the revolution of the universe, for even a part of the revolution is a time but it is not a revolution. Moreover, if there were several universes, time would be equally well the motion of each of them, so that there would be many times simultaneously. (Aristotle's rather summary dismissal of this view will be supplemented and confirmed by his later analysis. Aristotle himself speaks elsewhere [3] of a single universe, but this consideration is not relevant here.) Those who said that time was the sphere itself did so because all things are

[2] Cf. *ibid.*
[3] *On the Heaven* 276a18–279a11.

in time and likewise in the sphere of the universe. This view Aristotle considers too naive to require refutation. But since time seems to be chiefly a kind of motion or change, let us see whether such an approach is satisfactory. Motion and change are only in the thing which is moving or changing or where the thing may chance to be. (The latter Aristotle applies to locomotion, the former to other kinds of change.) But time is everywhere alike and is present to all things. Further, motion and change are faster and slower, but time is not. For faster and slower are determined by time, but time is not. Thus it is clear that time is not motion. Here Aristotle says that we shall for the present make no distinction between change (μεταβολή) and motion (κίνησις). (In general *change* is a wider term than *motion*. The latter includes increase and diminution, alteration, and locomotion. The former includes all these and the generation and destruction of a substance as well. But sometimes *motion* is extended to include generation and destruction. Since Aristotle explicitly states that the distinction between change and motion makes no difference for the analysis of time, the old controversy regarding this distinction in Aristotle's works is not relevant here.)

Now, continues Aristotle (218b21), even though time is not motion, it does not seem to take place without motion. For whenever there is no change in our thoughts or we are unaware of such change, it does not seem as if time had passed. This is just the case with the fabled sleepers in Sardinia whenever they awake. They connect the former and the later now to make a single now, having no consciousness of the intervening time. Just as if the now were not different but were one and the same there would not be time, so when the difference escapes us there does not seem to be any intervening time. If then our failure to notice time occurs whenever we distinguish no change, and the soul seems to abide in a single state, but we say time has passed whenever we perceive and distinguish change, it is clear that time is not without change. We come, therefore, to the tentative conclusion that time is neither motion nor something that exists without motion.

In our preliminary dialectical discussion we have been presented with difficulties about time that call for solution. Whatever we shall say later about time must be able to answer the questions thus raised. Can we justify the existence of time by specifying the manner in which it exists? With regard to the now we are faced with a dilemma. It cannot apparently be the same, and it cannot be different. Is it either or is it both? Since there seems to be a very close connection between time and the now, perhaps the answers to these questions will have much in common, and in answering one we shall perhaps answer the other. By raising these particular difficulties at the beginning Aristotle has opened a way to the very heart of the problem at hand, the nature of time. We can solve these difficulties only by determining what time is. Moreover, there are certain statements we have made about time that have to be justified by our subsequent discussion. We have said that the parts of time are not simultaneous. We have no objection perhaps to such a statement, since it appears to be true, but we shall have to see what basis it has in the very nature of time that we are attempting to discover. So we shall have to see why there cannot be several times that are simultaneous, why time can be everywhere present to all things, how time cannot be faster or slower, but is able to determine the speed of motion. The view of time that seems to be right, which we have been using in a vague way, has difficulties, the solution of which involves the very nature of time itself. But then, on the basis of the view of time that *seems* to be right, the traditional views of time have been shown to be inadequate. Our entire procedure will be justified if we examine this seemingly correct view of time and establish it on a scientific foundation. This we proceed to do by analyzing time into its principles. The dialectical portion of our argument has concluded and we begin to approach a positive and scientific view of the nature of time by seeing how time is related to motion, since that fact is already apparent.

### TIME AND MOTION

Since time, Aristotle proceeds (219a1), is not motion but is not independent of it, we who are seeking the nature of time must begin our investigation by grasping what time has to do with motion. For we perceive motion and time together. Even if there is darkness and we have no sensation whatsoever, but there is some motion present in the soul, along with this motion time seems to have passed. On the other hand, whenever time seems to have passed, so there seems to have been motion along with it. Our conclusion must be that since time is not motion it is something that belongs to motion.

In this latter section it is important to note just what Aristotle is doing, for it can easily be misunderstood. Bröcker remarks,

Die Bewegung in uns selbst, in unsern Vorstellungen, hat für uns eine ausgezeichnete Funktion. Denn ohne diese Bewegung ist für uns überhaupt keine Bewegung da. Jede andere Bewegung mag aufhören, es bleibt noch diese möglich, — aber wenn diese nicht ist, so ist für uns keine Bewegung zugänglich. Und wenn das der Fall ist, dann auch keine Zeit.[4]

[4] Walter Bröcker, *Aristoteles* (Frankfurt a.M.: V. Klostermann, 1935), p. 93.

But there is a misunderstanding here that Aristotle's express language does not warrant. The thesis of Aristotle in this section is simply that time is not independent of motion, as he states explicitly four times.[5] It is not his purpose to show that motion in the soul has an especially important position in our experience of time. He declares (218b29–219a1) that when we perceive motion we perceive time; when we perceive no motion we perceive no time. His conclusion is that time is not without motion. It is much the same as if I always perceive man as rational and never as not rational. My conclusion would be that man is rational. That is to say, my perception is only a means of judging what exists apart from my perception. There is, however, a difficulty with the perception of motion and time that complicates the situation. My very act of perception is a motion, and when I do not perceive there is no motion in the soul (218b30–32). That is why Aristotle says (218b21–23) that whenever there is no change in our thoughts or we are unaware of this change we have no perception of time. It is not that the change in our thoughts has an especial power to create a perception of time over and above change in general; it is rather that without this change in our thoughts there is no perception of any change at all. So Aristotle says (219a3–8) that we perceive time and motion together. It does not have to be a motion that we perceive outside of us. There has only to be motion in the soul to give rise to a perception of time. In this way he is saying that the motion we perceive in the soul is adequate to give rise to the perception of time; he is not saying that it is any better *as motion*, even though some kind of psychic motion is necessary for any act of perception.

The position of Bröcker (which helps to lead him astray

[5] 218b21, 218b33–219a2 (twice), 219a9–10.

in his subsequent discussion of the nature of time) arises in part from a misunderstanding of the course of the argument. We are beginning, in the Aristotelian analysis, more slowly and deliberately than he thinks. At a later stage of the argument Aristotle will discuss the relation of time to the soul. But before he can do that we must go through a great deal of examination of time itself. Then we are in a position to take up its relation to the soul and see if the perception on the part of the soul is necessary for time to *exist*. Here we are only concerned with the question whether there must be perception on the part of the soul for time to be *perceived*. The answer to this is obvious; there must be perception and we see that it always happens to be a perception of motion. We observe here that without a soul time cannot be perceived. We shall later ask if without a soul time can exist at all. This latter question does not concern us at this point of the argument because as a matter of fact we who are investigating what time is are students of nature who have souls and consequently are able to perceive time and motion. We ask what time is for us as investigators. Later we may be interested in asking what time would be if no soul existed to investigate it.

Now that time has been discovered to be connected in some way with motion, Aristotle proceeds to a closer analysis of the relationship (219a10). Since everything that is moved is moved over a certain magnitude, and every magnitude is continuous, motion, which corresponds to the magnitude, must be continuous. Since motion is continuous, the time of the motion must be continuous; for the length of time always seems to bear a definite proportion to the amount of motion.[6] Aristotle's treatment of magnitude and

---

[6] Two things are continuous when the touching limits of both are one and the same (227a11-12). The relation between the continuity and

motion here applies strictly only to locomotion, but we shall see that he does not intend to restrict time to locomotion. As Ross says,

μέγεθος is directly involved only in locomotion and in growth and diminution. But even in generation and destruction and in qualitative change there is involved a quasi-μέγεθος, an interval to be covered, and this equally with spatial μέγεθος is continuous.[7]

The "prior and posterior" is primarily in place by virtue of relative position.[8] Thus there comes about the contrast of prior and posterior in the motion which is over a certain magnitude, and from the motion prior and posterior comes about in time, since, as we have seen, time and motion are never without each other.[9] The prior and posterior in motion has motion as its subject, but the essence of prior and posterior is different from motion. This statement is very important for the distinction between time and motion. Motion as motion is the actualization of the potential. But the prior and posterior is essentially different, since it comes about from the relative position of the parts of the magnitude over which the motion takes place. Thus motion and the prior and posterior in motion are to be defined differently, although in subject they are the same. Time, we shall see shortly, is related to motion, not motion as such, but motion considered as having in it prior and posterior.

---

infinite divisibility of magnitude, motion, and time is discussed at length in *Physics* vi. 1–7.

[7] *Aristotle's Physics*, ed. W. D. Ross (Oxford: The Clarendon Press, 1936), p. 64.

[8] In *Categories* 14a26–29 the chief sense of "prior" is given as temporal. But that discussion simply observes and evaluates the meanings of terms as we use them. Here Aristotle is speaking as a physicist analyzing time into its principles and causes, and proceeding in this way he finds that in the order of nature time depends on position.

[9] Cf. *Metaphysics* 1020a26–32.

But, continues Aristotle, we recognize time whenever we distinguish a prior and posterior in motion. We say that time has passed when the soul perceives two nows, one prior, one posterior, with an interval between them. For that which is distinguished by the now seems to be time. But whenever we perceive the now as one, then time does not seem to have passed, since in that case there is no motion. We must perceive the now as prior and posterior in the motion, or perceive the now as the same but as related to something prior and something posterior. (These are two aspects of the same thing, as Aristotle makes clear later. We must not interpret the second alternative as do many commentators, such as Ross, "as an element (viz. the end) of an earlier section and an element (viz. the beginning) of a later." [10] For we are told explicitly [11] that we cannot in our reckoning of time accept the same now as the end of one period of time and the beginning of another.) Thus we arrive at our definition of time, the number of motion according to prior and posterior.

In arriving at this definition of time we have employed a typical Aristotelian procedure. In the dialectical discussion we saw that time seems above all to be a kind of motion. But it cannot be motion or, on the other hand, be without motion. When we began a positive approach to the problem we saw that time is not independent of motion, but must be something belonging to motion ($\kappa\iota\nu\eta\sigma\epsilon\omega\varsigma$ $\tau\iota$). At that moment we had come upon the matter or material cause of time, though we were not told that explicitly. Earlier thinkers who had identified time and motion had fallen into a common error from the Aristotelian point of view; they

---

[10] *Op. cit.*, p. 598. So also Carteron, "Aristoteles de Tempore," *Bulletin de la Faculté des Lettres de Strasbourg*, III (November, 1924), 32 f.
[11] 220a12–16.

had confused time with its material cause. To refute them on a scientific basis we have to show that there is another principle of time necessary for our understanding of it, the formal cause. We do not know what time is until our definition includes both the matter and the form. This point was emphasized when we noted that the prior and posterior in motion is not different in subject or matter from motion. But prior and posterior introduces a formal element that motion by its own definition does not have. It is this formal element that distinguishes time from motion, and we must bring it into our definition. So the perception of motion as such is not the recognition of time; there must be a perception of the prior and posterior in motion and a numbering process founded on this prior and posterior.

### TIME AS NUMBER AND AS MEASURE

Thus, continues Aristotle (219b2), time is not motion but that in virtue of which motion has number, that is, the numerable aspect of motion. That this is true is shown by the fact that we judge the more and less in general by means of number, but more and less motion by means of time. Now number may be spoken of in a twofold way. Number, on the one hand, may be that which is numbered or numerable, as ten men, or, on the other hand, that by means of which we number, as the abstract number ten. Time is number in the sense of that which is numbered; it is not an abstract number. For it is only the numerable aspect of motion, as the "tenness-of-the-men" is the numerable aspect of the ten men.

There is also another way in which time is spoken of by Aristotle. He frequently refers to it as the measure of motion. It might be well at this point to see how both terms apply to time and what is the distinction between them. We should note what Aristotle says elsewhere: quantity is defined as that which is divisible into components which are fitted to be individuals. A quantity is called plurality if it is numerable, a magnitude if it is measurable. A plurality is defined as that which is divisible into noncontinuous (that is, discrete) parts, a magnitude as that which is divisible into continuous parts, such as line, surface, and solid. Number is limited plurality.[12]

There is no difficulty, then, in seeing why time should be called a measure. Since motion is continuous and may be divided into continuous parts it is measurable, as a line is measurable, and Aristotle will later explain how motion is measured by time. The difficulty is in explaining how motion, which is continuous, can be numbered by time, which is also continuous. St. Thomas declares, "licet numerus sit quantitas discreta, tempus tamen est quantitas continua, propter rem numeratam; sicut decem mensurae panni quoddam continuum est, quamvis denarius numerus sit quantitas discreta."[13] But the problem is just why a continuous quantity can be called a *res numerata* instead of a *res mensurata*. The explanation of Simplicius misses the point in just the same way.[14]

We might be able to call time a number with some justification if we could find that it is in some way discrete. This is the case if we turn our attention to the now. We shall see that time is called a number of motion according to prior and posterior, not a measure of motion according to prior and posterior, although it is sometimes called a measure of

[12] Cf. *Metaphysics* 1020a7–14.
[13] *Commentaria in VIII Libros Physicorum Aristotelis*, Lib. IV, lect. xvii (*S. Thomae Aquinatis Opera Omnia*, II [Romae: Typographia Polyglotta, 1884], 203).
[14] *Simplicii in Aristotelis Physicorum Libros IV Priores Commentaria*, ed. Diels (Berolini: Typis et Impensis G. Reimeri, 1882), 714.4–12.

motion. The prior and posterior taken separately can be considered as two distinct nows. But the now is inextended and discrete, and as such may be looked upon as a number. Suppose I begin reckoning time from the present now. At certain intervals I count one minute, two minutes, three minutes, and so on. The lapse of an interval is denoted by an indivisible moment, the present now. When three such nows have been counted, as reckoned from the original now, we may say that the motion which is being reckoned can be represented or numbered consecutively by three units, each inextended and discrete, for each of the nows stands for a recurrence of some motion (as, for example, the hand of the clock counting off the minutes one by one).

But, it might be objected, the same could be said of the ten measures of cloth, or Simplicius' spear of eleven cubits. As we pass along from one cubit of the spear to the next, can we not allow the numbers one, two, three, and so on to stand for the points separating one cubit from the next? In that way we might be said to number the spear just as we have been said to number motion by means of time. We measure off the cubits on the spear by marking off points that are inextended and discrete, just as are the nows. Why must we be said to measure the spear and not number it, while we are able to number by means of time? Aristotle's reason for calling time a number may be explained by a statement he makes elsewhere, where he says that time does not consist of parts that have a definite position (*thesis*) with respect to one another, as a line does, though both are continuous. The parts of the line all exist together, but the parts of time do not. In this respect time may be said to resemble number. Moreover, time has a certain order (*taxis*), since one part is prior, one posterior. So in number two is prior to three, three to four.[15] In the light of this statement we may say that the spear of eleven cubits is not numbered because all eleven cubits exist at the same time. They are related one to the other by position, not by order. But the parts of time do not all exist together; they are related to one another by the order of prior and posterior. Thus time may be called the numerable aspect of motion, for motion is reckoned by means of successive nows, inextended like number and having among themselves the order that is possessed by number.

### TIME AND THE NOW

Proceeding to discuss the now (219b9), Aristotle first says that just as motion is always different so is time. This statement throws some light on what we have just said about time as a number. The order of prior and posterior in time comes about because in motion there is a prior and posterior. Motion, which is the actualization of the potential, takes place in various stages that correspond to the magnitude which is traversed by the motion. The motion does not exist with all its parts together; there is an order in the parts, and this order, insofar as it is made numerable by the now, is time.

We see, moreover, the importance of considering time a number only from the standpoint of prior and posterior when Aristotle goes on to say that all time that is simultaneous is the same, although it may be defined differently by the different events that are taking place in it . For it is the now that distinguishes time as prior and posterior, and the now is the same as subject, although it may be defined differently. That is to say, the now may be looked upon as the subject which has as its attributes the various events which

[15] *Categories* 5a24-33.

characterize it by taking place in it. But it is the now that distinguishes time as prior and posterior, and there is no difference in time except that of prior and posterior. Therefore, if events happen in the same now, that is, simultaneously, they are not prior or posterior to one another, but happen in the same time.[16]

When we consider the now in the flow of time, we find that it is in one sense the same, in another sense different (219b12). Insofar as it is differently located in the time series it is different, but in its substrate it is the same. To explain this we are reminded that motion corresponds to the magnitude, and time to motion. The moving body corresponds similarly to the point which we may suppose traces out the magnitude covered by the body in motion. It is by means of this body that we recognize the motion and the prior and posterior in it. Now this body as substrate remains the same (such as a stone in motion), but it may be considered different in definition as a body in motion (now here, now there). In the same way the sophists distinguish between Coriscus' being in the Lyceum and Coriscus' being in the marketplace. The moving body is different by being in different places. The now corresponds to the moving body, just as time corresponds to motion. For it is by means of the moving body that we recognize the prior and posterior in motion, and it is insofar as the prior and posterior is numerable that we have the now. So the now considered as substrate is always the same, for it is the prior and posterior in motion. But the being it possesses at various points in the time series is different, for it is insofar as the prior and posterior is numerable that we recognize the now. It is the now that is most knowable, just as motion is known through the moving body. For the moving body is an individual

---

[16] Aristotle returns to the problem of simultaneity later, 220b5-8.

thing, which the motion is not. So the now is in a sense the same, in another sense different, for the same is true of the moving body.

We note here the correspondence that exists for Aristotle in the magnitude, the motion, and the time. But the correspondence is shown by the introduction of new terms to be more complete than we were previously led to believe. We are given a kind of genetic approach to these three correlatives. The point is thought of as generating the line or magnitude, the moving body the motion, and the now time. The individual thing that we observe, of course, is the moving body. From our perception of this moving body, now at this point, now at that, comes the realization that motion is taking place. But in this very realization we have numbered the two nows and recognized that time has passed. Just as motion is recognized from perceiving the moving body at two different places, so time is recognized from perceiving the two nows, or the same now entering into two different relations, one prior, one posterior. We have finally answered our initial difficulty about the now. The moving body at two different places is the same *qua* moving body but different in position. It is the same moving body in its substrate but different in that the two phases are distinguishable by virtue of the order of prior and posterior. So the two nows that correspond to these phases are the same in substrate; they are the moving "prior and posterior." But insofar as this prior and posterior is numerable we recognize the difference in order and so perceive time. Thus from one point of view we have two different nows, from another the same now related to something prior and something posterior.[17] We begin to see that in answer to the initial questions about the existence of time, while we may

---

[17] As Aristotle himself has said explicitly, 219a31–32.

not dispel entirely the mystery of the manner in which time exists, we shall refer it to the more fundamental (for Aristotle) mystery of motion.

It is clear (219b33) that without time there would be no now, and without the now there would be no time. For just as the moving body and the motion accompany each other, so do the number of the moving body and the number of the motion. For time is the number of the motion, and the now corresponds to the moving body, and is like the unit of number.

This passage can be easily misunderstood. Ross says,

> The addition οἷον μονὰς ἀριθμοῦ is unfortunate, for a time is not made up of a finite number of nows, nor a movement of a finite number of positions, as a number is made up of a finite number of units. In fact the notion of the now as the unit of time is incompatible with the notion of it as the generator of time, which is that with which Aristotle has chiefly been working. The error is implicit in the original error of defining time as the number of movement.[18]

The explanation proposed by Simplicius is not very helpful. He says that just as the unit taken again and again makes number, so the now makes time, and the moving body the motion. But the unit, he amends, differs from the moving body and from the now in that it makes a discrete number, but they make continuous motion and time.[19]

These two points of view fail to see that time and the now may be considered in two ways, as was previously stated. Time may be thought of as a measure of motion. As such it is continuous because motion is continuous. From this standpoint the now may be considered the generator of time, just as the moving body generates the motion, and the point may

[18] *Op. cit.*, p. 601.
[19] Cf. *op. cit.* 726.6–13.

be supposed to generate the line. Aristotle's whole discussion of time and motion leaves us in no doubt that they are both continuous. But time and the now may from another standpoint be considered number, and Ross is right in saying that the now considered as the unit of number is consistent with time defined as number. It seems reasonable, however, to suppose that Aristotle called time a number for a definite purpose, even though he realized that time and motion are continuous. We saw that time may be called a number because only the now of time actually exists. It is inextended and discrete, and it has an order of prior and posterior with reference to other nows. These attributes make the definition "number of motion according to prior and posterior" altogether apt. Without forgetting that time and motion are continuous we may number time by means of the indivisible nows that the mind perceives. Corresponding to the now there is also a discrete aspect in the motion, namely, the indivisible phases to which the mind turns its attention when it numbers the motion. This does not make us declare that the motion is made up of a finite number of phases, or the time of a finite number of nows, because both motion and time are continuous. But motion has a numerable aspect, which we call time, because the mind can perceive these indivisible phases that exist not all at once but in a certain order, and number them by means of discrete nows. So time is constituted by nows, not as a continuum, but as number. The mind distinguishes indivisible nows in the continuous flow of time and allows each to stand for a number according to the order of prior and posterior in which they occur. That is why the now constitutes time, as the unit taken over and over again makes number; it is time considered as number, not as measure. Thus the now may be called the number of the moving object, and time the number of the motion. We recognize motion by perceiving the moving object at different phases and the time by perceiving different nows. So the now numbers the moving object by corresponding to these phases in the order in which they present themselves to the mind. The sum total of nows constitutes time as number by being the sum total of phases as distinguished by the mind in the continuity of motion.

The relation of the now to time continues (220a4). Time is made continuous by the now, and is divided at it. The same occurs in the case of the motion and the moving body. The motion is one because the moving body is one, not just as a single substance, a stone, for example (because the motion in the substance might have a lapse), but as a moving substance going through a single, uninterrupted motion. But, on the other hand, it is the moving body that distinguishes the motion as prior and posterior. We find the same situation in magnitude, where the point both connects the length of the line and divides it; for it is the beginning of one part and the end of another. Aristotle is saying that insofar as the now is connecting link time is an unbroken continuum. But when the now is considered as dividing the continuous flow of time, there occurs a numbering in accordance with the prior and posterior order of the nows. Thus time is the numerable aspect of motion.

When we take the same point in the line (220a12) and use it as two points, the beginning of one part and the end of another, a pause is necessary. The now, however, because of the motion of the moving body is always different. Consequently time is not number in the sense in which the same point on the line might be said to have a number, as beginning and end, but rather in the sense in which the extremities of a line might be called number.

Aristotle is here using the term "number" in a somewhat different sense in applying it to a line; his purpose is to illustrate how time is number by considering a line in analogous fashion. For all the points on the line exist simultaneously without any order of prior and posterior; consequently, the line would be measured, not numbered, although any measuring uses number.[20] But, accepting number in the sense in which it is used here, we see that a single point on the line does have plurality if it is considered the end of one part of the line and the beginning of another. The point can be numbered one, two, since two functions of the same point are distinguished by the mind. But this can be done only if the mind pauses at the point to make this distinction. This cannot be done with the now, says Aristotle, because in the flux of the nows there can be no pause. If the mind were to pause in an attempt to distinguish a single now, it would be able to think of it as the end of one period of time, or as the beginning of another, but while it was passing to the second function that now would have disappeared and another taken its place, with an infinite number of nows between the two. It is true, as Ross says, that we do seem to be able to pause over a now and consider it as the end of one period and the beginning of another.[21] But this would certainly not be considered time by Aristotle; it would be rather a frozen abstraction that could be called time only by a kind of equivocation. For it would destroy the distinction between the line of mathematics and the time of physics, the realities of mathematical science that

---

[20] Cf. *Metaphysics* 1052b20–24. Aristotle does not always strictly maintain the basic distinction between "numbered" and "measured" (*ibid.* 1020a7–14) since, in the nature of the case, any measuring process depends upon number. Conversely, cf. *ibid.* 1021a12–13, where "one" is said to be the beginning and measure of number.

[21] *Op. cit.*, p. 602.

are abstracted from all motion and those of nature that have in themselves as a distinctive feature a principle of motion.[22]

A single point on the line can have plurality because all parts of the line exist simultaneously. We can call the point one and two because it is the end of one part and the beginning of another, both of which exist simultaneously with the point. But the parts of motion do not all exist simultaneously. We number motion, as we have seen, by distinguishing indivisible phases in the motion that come into existence in an order of prior and posterior. We do not perceive the continuity of motion as if all its parts existed simultaneously, since motion by its very nature does not permit this. Consequently, we cannot number motion except by contrasting the present phase with another phase (that is held in the mind), between which two phases there is an infinite number of phases. This numerable aspect of motion according to the prior and posterior phases in the motion is time. Thus even if we could pause over a now and reckon it a plurality this would not be time, for there is no motion involved. As soon as motion is numbered there must be another now brought in that is contrasted with the first now. This is due, as Aristotle says, to the fact that the nows do not abide. They cannot be perceived all at once, as can the points on the line. There must be prior and posterior nows for the recognition of motion and time. Time is number, therefore, rather as the extreme points of the line are number (if we could call one point prior, another posterior), not as a single point might be said to be number. But we should not forget even then that the extreme points of the line exist simultaneously with the entire line, whereas the two nows and the

---

[22] On the distinction between the mathematician and the natural philosopher, cf. *Physics* ii. 2.

intervening time do not exist all at once; the analogy holds only to a certain point.

Moreover, time is not number in the same sense in which the parts of the line might be said to have number (220a16). For this statement Aristotle offers two reasons. The first is that, as we have just said, the middle point on the line may be used as two points if we make a pause at it, but this cannot be done with the now, since the nows are without pause. We may count the parts of a line and say that they are two in number. To do this both parts of the line must be perceived as existing simultaneously, so that the middle point is perceived as the end of one part and the beginning of another, and is consequently used as two points. But this cannot be done with time, if we take the dynamic view proposed by Aristotle. When we say that the games lasted two days, we do not hold the entire course of the games in mind simultaneously and perceive the two days as separated in the same way as we perceive the two parts of the line. This would be making nonsimultaneous things simultaneous and taking the now that divides the two days as something static, as indeed it would be making an entire motion static, something that motion cannot be. We must go back to the analogy of the extremities of the line. We mark off one day of the games by contrasting one now with a previous now, the second day by going through a similar process, that is, by considering end points, not middle points. For the motion is numbered only when nows are perceived in a certain order of prior and posterior; that is how they come into existence, not simultaneously.

The second reason why time is not number as the parts of the line might be said to have number is that the now is not a part of time any more than an indivisible phase is a part of the motion or the point a part of the line; only two lines can be parts of a line. This reason is obvious, since the now is indivisible and cannot be a part of time. But it clearly implies, as the first reason does not, that we number motion by means of the now, taking the indivisible, discrete nows as they present themselves to the mind, and giving them a number as they occur in the order of prior and posterior. When we number motion by means of the nows, it is understood that we distinguish the nows and realize that they are the limits of something that intervenes between them, the continuous flow of time.[23] The nows in themselves are only the number of the moving object (220a1–4). They provide the number of motion when we are conscious of the flow of time that is interrupted by them.

This discussion of the now is concluded with the statement that insofar as the now is a limit it is not time but only an attribute of time (220a21). But insofar as it numbers it is a number. For limits belong only to the thing of which they are limits, whereas number (ten, for example) is the number of these horses but belongs elsewhere as well.

This rather difficult passage may be interpreted in the light of some things we have seen.[24] Two nows bound a certain length of time, just as two points bound a line. But the nows, not being parts of time, are not time, any more than the points that bound the line are a line. For time and the line are continuous. So the now, insofar as it is a limit of time, is not time, but only an attribute of it. That is to say, the time has a certain length because the two nows that bound it are such a distance apart. But the now can be called a number insofar as it numbers something, and it numbers the moving body just as time numbers the mo-

---

[23] Cf. 219a25–30.
[24] Ross' reasons for thinking the text corrupt at 21–22 seem insufficient, especially since the reading is well supported.

tion.[25] There are consequently two points of view from which the now may be considered. It is the limit of the continuous quantity, time. It is also the number of the moving object, since the now corresponds to a certain indivisible phase of the moving object. To justify this distinction between the two functions of the now we are told that limits belong only to the thing of which they are limits; so the now as limit has reference only to time. But a number can be the number of many things; so the now considered as number has reference to everything that takes place in the now. As St. Thomas says, "nunc est terminus solius temporis, sed est numerus omnium mobilium quae moventur in tempore." [26]

### TIME AS THE SAME AND DIFFERENT

We have shown, says Aristotle (220a24), that time is the number of motion according to prior and posterior, and that it is continuous, being an attribute of something continuous. Thus we have looked upon time from two viewpoints, as the number of motion insofar as the nows are numbered according to the order of prior and posterior (with the consciousness, however, of the continuous flow of time between them) and as a continuum. We go on now to take up various attributes of time. In the first place, there is no minimum time, just as there is no minimum line, for both are infinitely divisible (220a27). Moreover, time is not called fast or slow, but it is spoken of as many or few and as long or short. Insofar as it is continuous we call it long or short; insofar as it is number, many or few (220a32).

---

[25] Ross' suggestion that we omit ἀριθμός and understand χρόνος ἐστί with Philoponus is poor (*op. cit.*, p. 603). The idea might be justified, although the now is strictly speaking not the number of motion and consequently not time. Reading ἀριθμός we do have a sufficient contrast with the first part of the sentence. The now is not time but it is a number.

[26] *Op. cit.*, Lib. IV, lect. xviii (207).

Thus Aristotle distinguishes between time as number and time as measure. We can speak of many days or few days, numbering time by means of regularly recurring nows, or as long or short, thinking of it as a continuous measure. But it is not fast or slow, any more than abstract number is fast or slow. We take up here the reason why we said previously that motion is faster or slower but time is not, for now we know that time is a number. The abstract number ten is not fast or slow; consequently ten men or ten days, insofar as they embody in concrete beings the abstract number, are not fast or slow. The ten men may be fast or slow, but not considered as numerically ten. Ten days can in no way be fast or slow, for they are nothing but the number of motion.

To continue, there is the same time everywhere at once, but not the same time prior and posterior, for the present change is one, but past and future change different (220b5). Time is not abstract number but rather that which is numbered. This is always different insofar as it occurs in the order of prior and posterior, for the nows are different. The number of a hundred horses and a hundred men is one and the same, but the things numbered are different.

This is an important passage for illustrating the Aristotelian method of argument. Some have thought that the one present change that Aristotle mentions is the revolution of the universe, on the basis of the later course of the discussion. This point of view, which is very widely held, is expressed thus by St. Thomas, "prima mutatio praesens, cuius primo et principaliter numerus tempus est, una est; sed huius mutationis altera pars est, quae iam facta est et pertransiit, et altera, quae futura est." [27] We shall see later that

---

[27] *Op. cit.*, Lib. IV, lect. xix (209). Bröcker, in stating (*op. cit.*, p. 101) that all present motions are unified by their reference to the soul, forgets that for Aristotle time and the now depend upon motion. The now is one because it corresponds to that motion (of any kind) which exists, as

this in a sense is true, but it is irrelevant at the present stage of the argument, for Aristotle is pursuing the investigation of time according to a definite plan. We are constantly reaching higher levels of analysis, but only toward the end do we come to the first motion of the heavenly sphere. On the present level there must be some meaning for the one motion that is intelligible in the context without going forward to a later stage of the argument.

We have said that time is the number of motion according to prior and posterior, and have been carefully told that time is not motion but the numerable aspect of motion (219b2–3). Now we find that there is the same time everywhere at once because the present change (or motion, since we are using the two without distinction) is one, but past and future time are not the same because past and future motion are different. Time is the numerable aspect, not of any one kind of motion, but simply of motion. Time is therefore the number of each and every kind of motion insofar as it is motion having prior and posterior.[28] Nor does it make any difference that there is variation within the same motion, such as faster and slower. Such variation does not alter the fact that it is motion, the actualization of something potential, and the numerable aspect remains the same. That is to say, the uniform flow of time is not affected by inconsistencies in the motion. Moreover, there is not a separate time for different kinds of motion. Finally, time is not differentiated by the simultaneous occurrence of individually different motions. For time is the number of motion according to prior and posterior, not according to simultaneous plu-

---

opposed to that which is no longer and that which is not yet. Surely it is a philosophical anachronism to introduce such a psychological unity into the physical time of Aristotle.

[28] Aristotle takes up this point at 223a29–b1.

rality. Time measures these individual motions, not insofar
as they are separate and individual, but insofar as they are
motions, and they are all equally motions. Thus time is the
number of motion as differentiated only by prior and posterior. The present motion, therefore, is one, though there
may be many motions differing individually and in kind and
having inconsistencies within themselves. For motion is one
thing, the actualization of the potential. Time numbers it
only insofar as there is an order of prior and posterior in it.
The prior and posterior is distinguished by the now, which
is the number of all existing motion. But the now is made
one because all existing motion is one *qua* motion. Past and
future time are different because in motion there is the order
of prior and posterior.

Abstract number, Aristotle continues, can apply to different things, such as ten horses and ten men, but the things
numbered are different. So a period of ten days will not be
the same time as another period of ten days, because time is
not an abstract number but it is that which is numbered.
One period of ten days will be of the same length as another such period, but they will not be the same time because one will be prior, the other posterior. But there is a
sense in which the same time can recur again and again, as
a year or a spring or an autumn (220b12), because the same
motion may repeat itself. So the years are repeated by the
repetition of a certain motion of the sun. But the years
differ numerically, though they are specifically the same,
just as the motion. For time numbers motion according to
prior and posterior.

### THINGS THAT ARE IN TIME

Not only do we measure motion by means of time, but
also time by means of motion, since they define each other

(220b14). Time defines motion by being the number of motion, but motion defines time as well, since we may call time much or little, measuring it by motion. In the same way we come to know the number by what is numbered, as for example the number of horses by one horse as the unit. We know how many horses there are by means of the number, and we know the number by using the one horse as the unit. So we measure motion by time and time by motion. This is only natural because the magnitude, the motion, and the time correspond to one another as continuous and divisible quantities. We measure magnitude by motion and motion by magnitude. We say that the road is long if the journey is long, and the journey long if the road is long. So it is with motion and time.

Time measures motion by determining a motion that will measure the whole motion, just as the cubit measures the length by determining an amount that will measure the whole length (221a1). So it is the unit of motion that is really the measure of motion, but time measures motion by determining the unit of motion. It is the function of the part to measure the whole (218a6–7), and only motion can be a part of motion. Similarly the cubit is not part of the length, but it measures the length by determining a part of the length that will be a measure.[29]

Time is the measure of motion, and for motion to be in time means that motion and its being are measured by time (221a4). Consequently, being in time for other things will mean that their being is measured by time. Other things are measured by time not as such but only insofar as their being involves motion.[30] But motion by its very nature possesses a being that involves motion; so time measures motion and

[29] This is all in accord with what is said at *Metaphysics* 1053a24–27.
[30] Cf. 221b19–20.

its being together. Now to be in time is either to exist when time exists or the same as to be in number. It cannot mean to exist when time exists because this is only incidental. To be in time as to be in number may mean that there are modes or attributes of time just as there are those of number. So the now and the prior are in time just as the unit and the odd and even are in number since time itself is a number. But apart from attributes, things themselves are in time just as they are in number. If this is so, they are contained in time just as things in number are contained in number and those in space are contained in space. Since things in time are so in the same way as things in number are so, a time greater than anything in time can be found (just as a number greater than anything in number can be found). Time is by its nature the cause of age and decay rather than the opposite, for time is the number of change, and change removes what is. Consequently, things that are always, insofar as they are always, are not in time. For they are not contained in time, nor is their being measured by time. This is made clear by the fact that they are not affected by time.

For Aristotle, therefore, the chief reason for saying that a thing is in time is that it is affected by time, that is to say, it changes; and insofar as it changes, its being is measured by time. Things that are in time generally pass away in time, and so we can say that there is a time greater than any of them. But motion is always for Aristotle, and is coextensive with time. It is in time because its being is measured by time, even though it is always. To be always, in the strict sense, so Aristotle indicates here, is not to be affected by time, not to have one's being measured by time, that is, to be unchanging.

Since time is the measure of motion (221b7) it is also the

measure of rest.[31] For all rest is in time. A thing has to be moved to be in motion, but not to be in time; for time is not motion but the number of motion. Not everything that is unmoved is at rest, but only that thing which is deprived of motion though capable of it.[32] Time measures what is moved and what is at rest insofar as it is moved or is at rest, for it measures the quantity of motion and of rest. It is not the quantity of the moving body simply that is measured, but rather the quantity of its motion. Things that are not moved or are not at rest are therefore not in time.

It is clear, then, that not every nonexistent thing is in time, namely, those nonexistent things that cannot exist, such as the commensurability of the diagonal of a square with the side (221b23). Time is in itself the measure of motion, and accidentally of other things (that is, the bodies that are in motion).[33] So a thing whose being is measured by time must have its being in motion or at rest, the privation of motion. Things that undergo perishing and becoming and,

[31] Ross may be right in bracketing κατὰ συμβεβηκός. The tradition is divided. He may not be right in believing Philoponus, who says that Alexander did not have the phrase (*Philoponi in Aristotelis Physicorum Libros V Posteriores Commentaria*, ed. Vitelli [Berolini: Typis et Impensis G. Reimeri, 1888], 756.7–9). Simplicius (*op. cit.* 758.6–8), in another context, indicates that Alexander had this expression. It is also difficult to see how Themistius is expanding, and we should probably consider him as supporting the reading (*Themistii in Aristotelis Physica Paraphrasis*, ed. Schenkl [Berolini: Typis et Impensis G. Reimeri, 1900], 156.8). Time is the measure of rest, but it would not be that unless there were some motion in existence of which time would be the number. So we might be justified in saying that time is the measure of rest accidentally. On this subject cf. *Metaphysics* 1032b2–6, where we read that in a sense contraries have the same form (*eidos*). For the being (*ousia*) of the privation is that of its opposite. Such is the case with health and sickness, since sickness is the absence of health, and health is the object of our knowledge and our definition. If we look forward to *Physics* 221b25–28 the things of which time is accidentally the measure seem to be contrasted with things that are in motion and at rest.

[32] Cf. 202a4–5.
[33] Cf. 221b16–20.

generally, those that exist at one time and not at another are
in time, for there is a time greater than their existence and
the time that measures their existence. Some nonexistent
things were at one time, others will be, depending upon the
direction in which time contains them. If time does not
contain things in either direction, these were not and they
will not be. Such are the nonexistents whose opposites are
always, as the incommensurability of the diagonal always is.
Neither this nor its opposite is in time (the one as always
existent, the other as always nonexistent). A thing whose
contrary is not always can be and not be, and there is
perishing and becoming of such things. Thus ends the discussion of things that are in time as measured by time.

## ATTRIBUTES OF TIME

We take up now the second meaning of being in time, the
way in which there are attributes of time just as the odd and
even are attributes of number (222a10). The now is a link
of time, for it connects past and future time, and it is a limit,
since it is the beginning of one part and the end of another.
This is not so clear as it is with the stationary point on the
line. The now divides time potentially, and as dividing the
now is always different. But insofar as it is a link it is always
the same. So it is with the point on the line. It is not always
one for the intellect, since it involves difference when the
line is divided. But insofar as it is one, it is the same in every
way. (That is, when we divide the line at the point, which
is a potential dividing place on the line, that point is no
longer one and the same for the intellect, but it is two points,
the beginning of one part and the end of another. If the
point is only a single point for the intellect, then it cannot
be considered as dividing the line. It is then the connecting
link as the beginning of one part and the end of another, but

does not have this twofold relation to the intellect.) So the now, continues Aristotle, in one way potentially divides time, in another is the limit of both parts and their unity. The dividing and the uniting are the same thing and occur in the same now, but they differ in essence. That is to say, dividing and uniting are accomplished by the same now, but they are differently defined.

We have here been concerned with time in its structure as a continuous quantity. It is made continuous by the now and is potentially divided by the now, as the line by the point. The now connects time since it is the end of one part and the beginning of another, and as connecting it is the same. This is not obvious with the now since it is always passing on, but we find that it is true nevertheless. On the other hand, if we consider that the now, being the end of one part of time and the beginning of another, is a potential dividing point, we are giving the now two functions with reference to the two parts that our process of division can make, although these were not actual parts before the division was made.

We should note that our discussion here is different from that at 220a9–18, where we said that the now could not be considered as the end of one part of time and the beginning of another. In that place we were not interested in the structure of time, but in time as number. When we number motion by means of time we cannot consider the same now two numbers as end and beginning, as we might conceivably do with the point. For we are numbering motion, which is ever changing, and the now does not remain long enough for us to use it as a number twice. But considering what time is in its structure as a continuum we find that the now must be both beginning and end. In numbering by means of the now we must use it as beginning or end; but we could not do this unless as the link of time it were both. The functional aspect of time is thus supplemented by a study of time's morphology.

A secondary use of the term "now" (222a21), when the time is near this primary now, is, "He will come now," because he will come today, or, "He came now," because he came today. "At some time" refers to a time delimited in relation to the now, for example, "At some time Troy was taken," or "At some time there will be a flood," for the time of these things is here delimited with reference to the now. If there is no time which is not "at some time" then every time must be delimited. Will time then ever fail? It will not, if motion always exists, and Aristotle believes that motion always exists. Is time always different or can the same time recur? Time in this respect is like motion. If the same motion recurs, then the same time recurs. Aristotle has already discussed this point (220b9–14): the same individual motion cannot recur, for there would be the difference of prior and posterior, but the same motion specifically can recur, as the completion of the sun's annual journey through the zodiac. So time, being that which is numbered, cannot recur except for a time that is specifically the same, as a year. The two questions he has asked Aristotle answers in terms of the now (222a33). Since the now is the end of past time and the beginning of future time, just as the circle has convexity and concavity in the same thing, so in the now time is always at a beginning and at an end. On this account time always seems to be different, for the now is not the beginning and end of the same thing. Moreover, time cannot fail, for it is always at a beginning.

Continuing his treatment of the attributes of time, Aristotle says that "presently" or "just" (in Greek the same word, ἤδη) refers to a part of future or past time which is near the indivisible present now, for example, "I shall walk presently," or "I have just been walking." "Lately" also refers to the part of past time that is near the now; so, "I went lately." But "long ago" refers to the long distant past. "Suddenly" refers to something that has left its former state in a time that is imperceptibly small. It is the nature of change to remove all things from their former state, for change is the cause of perishing rather than of becoming. Change in itself removes what is and only incidentally is the cause of becoming and being. Strictly speaking, time is not even the agent of destruction, because even this change takes place incidentally in time.[34] So, concludes Aristotle, we have shown that time exists and what it is, and how we are to speak of the now and other temporal terms.

### THE UBIQUITY OF TIME

When we have made these distinctions, declares Aristotle (222b30), it is clear that every change and everything that changes is in time, for all change is perceived to be faster or slower. A thing is said to move faster when the completion of its change is prior to the completion of another change (supposing they change over the same interval and with a regular movement, as, in the case of locomotion, on the circumference of a circle or along a straight line). But what is prior is in time; for we say prior and posterior only with reference to the distance from the present now. Since the now is in time, so prior and posterior will be in time, for the distance from the now will be in that in which the now itself is, namely, time. Since every motion, therefore, in-

---

[34] Cf. St. Thomas, *op. cit.*, Lib. IV, lect. xxii (220), Ex hoc enim ipso quod aliquid movetur, recedit a dispositione quam prius habebat. Sed quod perveniat ad aliquam dispositionem, hoc non importatur in ratione motus inquantum est motus, sed inquantum est finitus et perfectus.

volves a prior, and since the prior is in time, it is evident that all change and motion are in time.

We should note here that we are using "prior" and "posterior" for the first time with exclusive reference to time. There is prior and posterior in time because there is prior and posterior in motion, as we have seen before. But once we find the prior and posterior in time we can use it to compare the faster and slower in motion, as we do here. Thus we finally establish our right to judge the speed of motion by time that we previously assumed (218b13–17) and partially confirmed when we said that time, being number, is not fast or slow (220a32–b5).

We may now ask (223a17) why time is thought to be in everything, in earth and in sea and in heaven. Is it because time is an attribute or condition of motion, being the number of motion, and all these things are capable of motion, since they are all in place? Is it that time and motion are together in respect of both potentiality and actuality?

This passage offers difficulty in interpreting the meaning of the way in which time and motion are together in respect of both potentiality and actuality. This is explained by Ross, "the things that are actually in movement are identical with those that are actually in time, and those that are potentially in movement with those that are potentially in time." [35] But this does not explain the passage. Ross is right in rejecting the suggestion that things which are potentially in motion and potentially in time are things at rest, for things at rest are actually in time (221b7–23). He thinks Simplicius may be right in believing that Aristotle means things that have not yet come into existence, but can do so.[36] But this reference seems irrelevant here. A satisfactory inter-

---

[35] *Op. cit.*, p. 610.
[36] Simplicius *op. cit.* 758.2–3.

pretation seems to be that suggested by St. Thomas, "tempus est simul cum motu, sive motus accipiatur secundum actum sive secundum potentiam." [37] Though restricting the potentiality and actuality to motion alone is not immediately suggested by the statement of Aristotle, it is an altogether possible reading. In this case, of course, the things that are potentially in motion are those that are at rest; but they are actually in time. It should be noted that Aristotle uses κινητά, things that are movable, though not necessarily in motion. All these things are movable, says Aristotle, because they are in place. That is to say, everything in the universe has change of position, even if it has no other change.[38]

TIME AND THE SOUL

One might also ask (223a21) whether there would be time or not, if there were no soul. If there cannot be some being that will number there cannot be anything that is numerable. Therefore there can be no number; for number is that which is numbered or that which is numerable. But if nothing other than soul and in the soul intellect is able to count, then there cannot be time if there is no soul. There would be only the substrate of time, namely, motion, if motion can exist without soul. The prior and posterior is in motion and, as numerable, constitutes time.

The relation of time to the soul is dismissed thus briefly

---

[37] *Op. cit.*, Lib. IV, lect. xxiii (222).

[38] The fifth bodily substance of which the heavenly bodies are composed is exempt from generation and destruction, increase and diminution, and alteration (*On the Heaven* 270a12–14). But it has change of place, for all natural bodies are capable of locomotion (*ibid.* 268b14–16). The first heaven is not in place except indirectly, that is, only because its parts are in place; so its spherical motion is strictly a movement of the parts (*Physics* 212b8–11). Simplicius quotes some interesting statements of Alexander on this subject and adds a few of his own, *op. cit.* 758.17–27.

by Aristotle because whether or not there could be time without the soul is not a real concern to the student of nature. For when we begin to investigate nature and the part played by time in nature and in motion, we do so as beings who possess souls, and we find that time is that aspect of motion by virtue of which motion presents itself to us as numerable. Asking what time would be if there could be no soul to number motion is somewhat irrelevant to the present analysis, and Aristotle passes lightly over it. Our previous discussion, of course, presupposed that there was a soul to number motion. As a matter of fact, it gave the soul a more important position than is at first evident. For we can number motion by means of the nows only if the mind contrasts the present now with nows that have gone into the past. To perceive an order in the nows and number motion accordingly demands that there be some recollection of the nows that are no longer in existence. But the process by which the mind does this does not belong in natural philosophy, and Aristotle passes over the psychological aspect of time, which was later to be stressed by St. Augustine. The prior and posterior in motion is not time except so far as it is numerable. But it cannot be numbered if a being does not exist to number it. Thus without a being to number the prior and posterior there can be nothing numerable and consequently nothing that has been numbered. Since time is a numbered number, there cannot be time without a being to number the prior and posterior. If only the intellect, then, is capable of numbering, there can be no time without an intellectual soul, but only motion, the substrate of time. These further questions Aristotle deems irrelevant, since they have nothing to do with the nature of time as considered in natural philosophy.

### TIME AS THE NUMBER OF ALL MOTION

We continue with the statement that time is the number of continuous motion simply, and not of any particular kind of motion (223a29). For all kinds of motion take place in time, becoming and perishing, increase, alteration, and locomotion. It is therefore only so far as each of these is motion that time is the number of each. This explicit declaration confirms what has been strongly implied throughout our discussion, especially where we were told that present change is one (220b6–7).

An objection is now raised (223b1). It is possible for more than one motion to be going on simultaneously. Since time is the number of each and every motion, is it not possible for two equal times to exist simultaneously? (Two unequal times can exist simultaneously in a sense, as a year and a day within the year.) There cannot be two equal and simultaneous times, answers Aristotle, for these would be one and the same time. Even times that are not simultaneous can be the same, but only in species.[39] Suppose there are seven dogs and seven horses; they differ, but they have the same number. In the same way motions that have simultaneous limits have the same time, though one may be fast, another slow, one locomotion, another alteration. Consequently, there may be many different motions, but time is everywhere the same because the number of equal and simultaneous motions is everywhere one and the same.

The analogy of the seven dogs and the seven horses is not meant to illustrate how different times can be the same in species, but rather how motions that are different but never-

---

[39] Cf. 220b12–14. This point is taken up in a more elaborate way at 224a2–15, where he indicates that in the cycle of time the same time, such as a year, may repeat itself, but not the same year.

theless have simultaneous limits have one and the same time
as their number. Ross' interpretation is influenced by a
similar analogy at 220b10–12, where the purpose is different.
Aristotle is not intending to say, of course, that time is an
abstract number, but it has certain resemblances to abstract
number.[40] Looking beyond the analogy given here by Aristotle we see that the reason why different motions that
possess simultaneous limits have the same time as their number is that time is the measure of each motion insofar as each
is motion (223a32–33), and present motion is one (220b6–
7). Unless motion were in some way one it would be useless
to speak of different motions as having simultaneous limits;
for the limits are simultaneous only because they occur in
the same now. But the now is one because it is the number
of existing motion, which is one so far as it is motion. Thus
we affirm once more that time is the same everywhere at
once.[41]

We have seen (221a1–2) that time measures motion by
determining some motion that will measure the whole motion, for the measure must always be like that which it
measures. Now we are told (223b13) that everything is
numbered by some one thing that is like it, as units by a
unit, and horses by a horse. So time is numbered by some
determined time. But how are we to arrive at a determined
time? Time is measured by motion just as motion is measured by time, since by means of a motion which is determined by time we measure the quantity of both motion and
time.

[40] There is another parallel at 220b3–5. But at 220b10–12 the analogy is
intended to show that times that are not simultaneous may be reckoned
by the same abstract number, such as ten days; these are only specifically
the same, not individually the same, because time is not abstract number
but that which is numbered. Cf. Ross, *op. cit.*, p. 391.
[41] Cf. 220b5–6; also 218b13 and 223a17.

We should note here that units are *numbered* by a unit, and time by a determined time, but time is *measured* by motion. We thus preserve the distinction that has been maintained throughout our discussion, though sometimes the distinction is not altogether obvious. Just as time measures motion by determining some motion that will measure in turn the whole, so motion measures time by determining some time that will measure the whole. But of course this motion too is determined by time, since time is the measure of motion. The reciprocity of measure should not be disturbing, for the ten horses are numbered by the number ten, and we arrive at the number ten in this instance by using one horse from the ten as the unit of measurement. Time and motion are similarly the measure of each other, though time primarily of motion. The time, for example, involved in the sidereal day is the measure of the motion of a star from one transit of the meridian to the next, but in turn this motion determines the length of the sidereal day and is a check on our chronometers, and still further by means of our chronometers we can detect a slight variation in the length of the sidereal day and offer as explanation the shrinkage of the earth or some other cause. Thus by constantly measuring one thing against another we arrive at greater accuracy.

If, then, that which is primary is the measure of everything like it, uniform circular motion is above all the measure of time, because its number is best known (223b18). Alteration, increase and becoming are not uniform, but locomotion is. We shall later see Aristotle's reasons for saying that only locomotion is uniform, and of locomotion only that which is circular. We note here that circular motion is above all the measure of time because it is primary, uniform, and best known.[42] In our present discussion there is a close connection between being primary and being best known. The view of Simplicius is that a time which will measure all time must be the time of a motion that will measure all motions. Such a motion must be primary, uniform, and known; otherwise it will be useless as a measure.[43]

There is a strong tendency among commentators to think of circular motion as primary and best known because the motion of the heavens is the first motion and that which is most obvious to men.[44] But Aristotle later takes pains to show that circular motion is primary for reasons that are not at all obvious to men as a whole. If the ideas of "primary" and "best known" are linked together here, it is reasonable to suppose that circular motion is best known for the same reasons that it is called primary, and these reasons do not involve observation of the heavens as part of the argument. It seems probable that the number of circular motion is best known by nature, not best known to men, to use the distinction put forward in the *Physics* [45] according to which we are said to proceed in our study of nature from things that are better known to us to those that are better known by nature (though we might better express the idea by "more knowable"). Since circular motion will be shown to be primary, and not primary in the sense that we know it first, we should expect this to be the meaning of "best known" here. To say that it refers to the motions of the heavenly bodies, by which men have determined periods of time, is to introduce something extraneous into the argument. The

---

[42] Cf. *Metaphysics* 1052b20–1053b8, where the nature of the measure is discussed, and we are told that the measure is that by which each thing is known primarily.

[43] *Op. cit.* 768.1–6.

[44] This may be noted already in the statements of Simplicius and in those of Alexander which he reports, *ibid.* 768.28–769.4.

[45] 184a16–21.

motions of the heavenly bodies have nothing to do with the fact that circular motion is primary, and probably nothing, therefore, with the intrinsic knowability of its number.

This interpretation may seem to be contradicted by what Aristotle goes on to say (223b21). Since circular motion is primary, he says, some have thought time to be the motion of the sphere, since other motions and time as well are measured by this motion. To understand Aristotle's meaning, however, we must first realize that as a matter of fact men do determine their periods of time by the motions of the heavenly bodies, chiefly by what appears to be the revolution of the sphere of the universe. One explanation of this fact is that the revolution of the sphere may be time, as had been said. Aristotle disagrees with this point of view, though he does not doubt that the motion of the heavenly sphere does indeed measure other motions and time itself. But he is attempting an explanation that has its basis in the very idea of time as the number of motion, his own definition. It would not do to say that time is measured primarily by circular motion because men in fact measure time by the motion of the sphere. There must be something in the nature of time and motion themselves that leads us to believe that circular motion is primarily the measure of time. This, Aristotle declares, is the fact that time is measured by motion and primarily by the primary motion, which he later proves to be circular motion. The common measurement of time by the motion of the sphere does not prove the point for Aristotle; it merely indicates that men in general vaguely realize the truth of what he is trying to prove scientifically. The same may be said of the philosophical view that time is the motion of the sphere; it is extraneous evidence that there is a close connection between time and circular motion.

Aristotle continues to give evidence that men recognize

that there is this relationship between time and circular motion (223b23). There is the common saying that human
affairs form a circle, and that there is a circle in other things
that have a movement according to nature. All such things
are discriminated by time and have their beginning and end
as though conforming to a kind of cycle. For even time
itself is thought to be a kind of circle; the reason for this is
that time is the measure of this kind of motion, and is itself
measured by it. To say that the things that come into
existence form a circle is to say that there is a circle of time,
and this is to say that time is measured by circular motion.
(We should note that the evidence given here by Aristotle
is to show that there is a connection between time and circular motion as such, not the circular motion of the sphere.)

### SUPPLEMENTARY CONSIDERATIONS

The last four books of the *Physics* take up a classification
of motions in detail, and time enters into the discussion frequently. There are several points that are relevant to our
discussion, especially a number of arguments that will supplement well our previous consideration. Aristotle emphasizes frequently that time and motion are both infinitely
divisible, as may be said for all continuous quantities.[46] At
233a21–31 one of Zeno's paradoxes is handled neatly, if we
consider that Aristotle is refuting it according to the form
in which it was put. Zeno had apparently said that if motion
is possible then a thing can pass over an infinite number of
points in a finite time, which is impossible. Aristotle admits
that in a finite time a thing cannot come into contact with
things that are quantitatively infinite; but it can come into
contact with things that are infinite in respect of divisibility,
as are the points on the length of a line. For time is also

[46] An especially interesting argument is at 232b26–233a12.

infinite in this respect, and the moving body comes into contact with points that are infinite in a time that is infinite in the same sense. Aristotle insists elsewhere (263b3–6) that it is possible to pass through an infinite number of points either of time or of distance only if the points are potential, not actual.

At 233b33–234a24 the now is shown to be indivisible in its function of dividing past and future. The extremity of both times must be the same, for if the extremity of each were different then there would be time between them, which would of course be divisible. On this assumption the now would be divisible, and in the present now there would be both past and future. There cannot, therefore, be motion or rest in the now (234a24–34). For if motion could be in the now, this would make the now divisible, which we have proved to be impossible. But if there can be no motion in the now, there can be no rest, for only that can be at rest which can naturally be in motion, and a thing cannot naturally be in motion in the now. Moreover (239a14–17), when we say that a thing is at rest we imply that the thing is in the same state as it was previously; thus two nows, not one, are needed to determine rest. This statement is interesting in view of the fact that we have said that time numbers motion not as a single point on the line, but as the extremities of the line (220a14–16). To recognize motion we must perceive two different phases of the moving thing; the same applies to the thing at rest.

In the eighth book Aristotle shows that locomotion is the primary kind of motion. If we first consider increase, alteration, and locomotion, we find that locomotion is primary. There cannot be increase without alteration, for that which is increased, though in one sense it is increased by what is like itself, in another is increased by what is unlike itself.

But increase is brought about only by things becoming like to like. Alteration is necessary, then, insofar as there is this change from contrary to contrary. But if the food is altered there must be something that alters it and makes the potentially hot actually hot. Consequently, that which alters it must be at one time nearer to and at another farther from that which is altered. But this cannot be without locomotion (260a26–b6). Generation may seem first of motions since the thing must first be generated. This is true of any single generated thing, but there must be a prior thing in locomotion, which is not being generated (261a4–7). Moreover, that which is being generated is imperfect and is moving toward a first principle; so what is posterior in the order of generation is prior in the order of nature. Now all things that undergo generation acquire locomotion last. Thus locomotion is prior to other motions in respect of perfection (261a13–20).

Only locomotion can be continuous. All other motions and changes are from opposite to opposite; being and not-being are the limits of becoming and perishing; contrary qualities, of alteration; greatness and smallness, of increase and diminution. Opposite changes are changes to opposite limits. Now opposite changes must have an interval of time between them, for otherwise opposite changes will belong to the same thing at the same time. If, for example, white changes to black and then black to white in the same thing, there must be an interval during which there is black and no change is occurring; otherwise white will be changing to black at the same time as black is changing to white. The time interval in such changes prevents the change from being continuous (261a31–b7).

Moreover, rectilinear motion cannot be continuous. It is impossible to move along an infinite straight line, since no such thing exists, and if it did it could not be traversed. But when motion along a finite straight line turns back, it is really two motions, not a single continuous motion (265a17–21). Moreover, rectilinear motion has a beginning, middle, and end all in itself, points where the body must start and finish; but in a circle these are not determined, so that the moving body is always and never at a beginning and at an end (265a27–b1). Circular motion is prior to all other motions and changes, for a motion that can be eternal is prior to one that cannot. Only circular motion can be eternal, for every other must be interrupted by an interval of rest (265a24–27). Circular motion alone can be uniform. Things in rectilinear motion do not move uniformly from beginning to end, but all things move faster in proportion as they are farther from the state of rest. But circular motion alone has neither beginning nor end within itself (265b11–16). Thus circular motion is the primary kind of motion.

This, then, is the reason that circular motion is said by Aristotle to be above all the measure of time. It is the primary motion and as such is the measure of all other motion. It is moreover the only motion that is continuous in the full sense of the word, and the only one that is uniform. All these characteristics make it most worthy of being the measure of all motion, and consequently of time as well. On the other hand, since circular motion is primary, time will primarily be the measure of this motion. There is an interesting statement at 265b8–11, where Aristotle is trying to show that circular motion is primary. Since circular motion, he says, is the measure of motions, it must be primary, for all things are measured by that which is primary; and because it is first, it is the measure of the others.[47]

Here, it seems, Aristotle is making use of the common

[47] Cf. *On the Heaven* 287a23–24.

fact that men measure motions by the circular motion of the heavens to show that circular motion is primary, since all things are measured by what is primary. On the other hand, because circular motion is primary, it is naturally fitted to be the measure of the others. That is to say, the argument of Aristotle is convertible with qualification. The first part is meant to prove that circular motion is primary by the fact that one instance of it is used as measure; we are arguing from what is posterior in nature to what is prior. The second part presents what is true in the nature of things; because circular motion is primary, it is the measure of the others. Again we should observe that the circular motion of the heavens does not make circular motion the primary motion in the argument. Rather, as Aristotle puts it (260a21–26), if there is some motion that is primary and continuous, this is the motion that is imparted by the prime mover (on the first heaven). Aristotle may be influenced by his observation of the heavens, to be sure, but his arguments are intended to stand on their own merits.

### THE ULTIMATE CAUSE OF TIME

We have formulated the definition of time and discussed various problems concerning time without offering the ultimate cause for the existence and nature of time. This ultimate cause is suggested at the end of the *Physics* (267b24–25), where it is said that the prime mover causes an everlasting motion and causes it during an infinite time. Without taking up problems that are beyond the scope of this study, it might be well to look briefly at other treatises of Aristotle which give us relevant information. We read first that the continuity of motion and of time is caused by the body which moves in a circle,[48] and then that this body

---

[48] *On Coming to Be and Passing Away* 337a32–33.

is the heaven whose unending motion embraces the infinity of time.[49] Outside the heaven there is neither place nor time, and the fulfillment of the heaven includes all time and infinity, for its circular motion is unceasing.[50]

In arriving at the ultimate cause of time, which is the unceasing circular motion of the first heaven as effected by the influence of the prime mover exerted at the circumference,[51] we now perceive why time exists and why it has the characteristics that we discussed earlier. Time is, for example, continuous and uniform because of the unending motion of the heaven, and time is one everywhere because all motions are ultimately contained in this one perfect motion.[52] We even find that on this higher level of analysis Aristotle reminds us of Plato in relating time to eternity; he indicates that there is an eternal cause of time outside the universe, and, moreover, that the unending motion of the heaven through infinite time is an approximation to the eternal perfection of the cause.[53] Nevertheless, in Aristotle's treatment of time we are given a series of literal statements that add to our knowledge of time in deliberate and measured fashion, and each stage of the argument is self-sufficient and intelligible in itself. As the analysis proceeds by rising to the ultimate cause of time, our knowledge is increased but our previous results are still valid. Aristotle begins characteristically by relating time to motion with the most simple and sparing use of terms, but ends by setting forth a world-view of time that in its universality and solemnity is akin to that of Plato's *Timaeus*.

[49] *On the Heaven* 283b26–284a6.
[50] *Ibid.* 279a11–b3.
[51] *Physics* 267b6–9.
[52] *On the Heaven* 279a28–30, 284a3–11.
[53] *Ibid.* 279a18–b3, *Metaphysics* 1072a21–26; cf. *Physics* 267b22–26.

# 3

# PLOTINUS

## *Time, the Life of Soul*

PLOTINUS considers time most fully in the seventh treatise of the third *Ennead*, "On Eternity and Time." Although his conceptions of eternity and time play an important part in his entire system, it is here that he arrives at the proper definition of time by what he considers the proper method of approach, and it is here that he considers most carefully the discussions of Plato and Aristotle. What Plotinus says of time in other places will of course throw light on the present treatise. But it is most important to examine carefully the continuity of method and the results it produces in the one treatise where Plotinus proposes to discover the essential nature of time.[1]

### THE NATURE OF ETERNITY

We realize, says Plotinus (1. 1),[2] that time and eternity are different, and that one has reference to the sphere of

[1] Jean Guitton, *Le temps et l'éternité chez Plotin et saint Augustin* (Paris: Boivin et Cie., 1933), discusses this treatise rather briefly, but considers at length the historical and psychical implications of time in other treatises. A generally good treatment of this treatise is that of Gordon H. Clark, "The Theory of Time in Plotinus," *The Philosophical Review*, LIII (1944), 337–358.

[2] Chapter and line references for this treatise are to *Plotin, Ennéades*, ed. Bréhier, Vol. III (Paris: Société d'Édition "Les Belles Lettres," 1925).

becoming and the sensible universe, and the other to the everlasting nature. We seem thus to have a spontaneous knowledge of them by a grasp of intuition. But we have difficulty when we try to understand them by a closer approach. We are tempted to look at the various explanations offered by the ancients and deem it sufficient to know what they said, without pursuing the matter any farther for ourselves. We should believe, to be sure, that some of the ancients of happy memory discovered the truth; but nevertheless we should inquire who were the most fortunate and how we too can come to an understanding.[3] First we should make inquiry about eternity; for if we know what the unchanging model is, perhaps we can thereby arrive at a knowledge of its image, which we call time. But it would also be possible before one contemplated eternity to have some notion of time and proceed thence by reminiscence to a contemplation of that to which time has been likened, if indeed it is true, concludes Plotinus, that time does bear such a resemblance to eternity. This resemblance of time to eternity, which Plotinus takes from Plato, receives ample confirmation later in this treatise.

In considering what is the nature of eternity, Plotinus first examines two proposals (2. 1). In the first place, eternity might be the intelligible essence itself. This is analogous to the view that time is to be identified with the heaven. Secondly, eternity might well be identified with rest in the intelligible world, just as in the sensible world some have thought that time is motion. These suggestions Plotinus dismisses for a variety of reasons. It is true that the intelligible essence contains the same things as eternity. But essence contains them as its parts, while eternity is present

---

[3] Plotinus believes in an independent spirit in search of the truth, though consideration is to be given to the ancients, especially Plato.

to all eternal things as a whole. Moreover, eternal could not be predicated of essence if eternity and essence were identical, as when Plato says that the nature of the model was eternal.[4] Similarly, eternity cannot be identical with rest, for we could not then say that rest is eternal. Moreover, eternity must not only be at rest, but possess unity and be without extension. But rest, insofar as it is rest merely, does not imply the notion of unity and lack of extension.

What then, asks Plotinus (3. 1), is this character of the intelligible world by virtue of which it is called eternal and everlasting? It is something that is in a sense one, but in another sense a compound of many things. It is a nature that in some way accompanies the beings of the intelligible world, or is joined to them, or is perceived in them. If one considered this multiple power of the intelligible world, then one might call it being so far as it is substrate, motion so far as it possesses life, rest so far as it is unchanging, difference and identity so far as these several things form a unity.[5] But if we are to see eternity as it is we must unite these several things into the unity that they really are in the intelligible world. This would be the peculiar life of the ideal world. We must join together the difference and the unceasing activity and the identity and the life that does not pass from one thing to another, but is unchanging and without extension. Then we see eternity as the life that is forever unchanging and possesses all its reality in the present. There is no succession involved in this life, since nothing has passed and nothing is to come, but whatever it is it is

---

[4] *Timaeus* 37d. So in vi. 2. 8 Plotinus declares that being, motion, and rest in the intelligible realm are three distinct things since we can think of each separately.

[5] Plotinus discusses the five genera, which have their source in Plato's *Sophist*, in vi. 2.

always. Thus eternity is not the substrate (though, as we have seen, this is one aspect of it), but rather a kind of radiation of the substrate that goes forth from it by virtue of the identity it possesses in being that which is, not that which is to come. Since there is nothing that it can come to possess that it does not already possess and nothing that it loses of what it possesses, we cannot say of it that it was or will be, but only that it is. Thus we find that eternity is the life of being in its very being, at once whole, complete, and entirely without extension.

Plotinus then approaches eternity from a different point of view to insist that we should not consider it to be in any way accidental to the intelligible essence (4. 1). Rather eternity comes from it and exists in union with it. If the intelligible essence is to be a whole in the true sense of the word, then it must not only be all things, but must lack nothing. Consequently there is no future for it, for if there were that would imply that it lacked something. If the future were taken away from things that become they would straightway lose their being. But if a future were added to things that are not subject to becoming, they would be removed from the rank of true beings; for being would not be their natural possession if it appeared in coming to be and in progress to the future. The being of things that become continues from the first moment of their generation to the last, at which time they cease to be. This kind of existence demands a future, and if this future is taken away their life and their being are diminished. So the sensible universe has a future toward which it hastens, drawing being to itself by producing one thing after another and moving in a circle through a kind of striving for real being.[6] And this is the cause of the motion that seeks eternity in

[6] This revolution of the heaven Plotinus discusses more fully in ii. 2. 1.

the future. But the true beings have no desire of the future, for they are already complete and possess all the life that we may say is due them. Thus intelligible essence is complete not only in the sense that it comprehends all being, but also in the sense that it can never lack anything or contain any not-being. This state and nature of essence would be eternity, for eternity is that which is always.

Plotinus now considers eternity from the standpoint of one who contemplates it. A thing may be called eternal if I can see that it is of such a kind that it has never suffered any change (5. 1). It may be called everlasting if its nature is such as to offer the assurance that there is no possibility of change for it. Imagine the state of one who unceasingly contemplates eternity and through this contemplation, achieved by an eternal principle within himself, becomes like it and eternal. (It is upon Plotinus' conviction that there is such an eternal principle within us that his statements about eternity are based.) Suppose that a being of this kind is eternal, one who does not fall away to another kind of nature, who possesses a life that is ever complete, with never an addition. Such a being possesses everlastingness, which is an attribute of the substrate, arising from it and existing in it. Eternity is the substrate of this everlastingness, Plotinus now affirms, together with this attribute that is seen in it. Eternity (to which the one who contemplates it may be assimilated) thus may well be called God making himself manifest as he is, a being without change or difference and having steadfast life. If we say that eternity consists of many things, that should not cause wonder, for each of the intelligible beings is many by virtue of infinite power. The infinite is that which can never fail, and this is especially true of eternity, since it spends none of itself. We may say, therefore, that eternity is infinite life that is ever complete and spends none of itself because none of it has passed and none is still to come. This, concludes Plotinus modestly, would be close to a definition of eternity.

Plotinus now proceeds to explain certain statements made about eternity by Plato (6. 1). The eternal nature is centered in the One, arises from it, and is turned toward it. For this reason Plato speaks of eternity as abiding in One. For being thus abiding, as the act of a life that is abiding by being turned toward the One and in the One, this eternity is true being and true life. For true being is that which is never not-being or being in another way. It is without change or succession and is not subject to extension, evolution, or progression. There is in it no prior and posterior, and the statement that it is is the truest thing that can be said about it, and in fact is its very self. Thus we are led once again to eternity. It is that which is, and this uniform self-identity Plotinus has demonstrated by taking the Platonic concept of unity in the *Timaeus* [7] and transferring it to his first hypostasis, the One, which is the source of all being as the source of all unity and goodness, but is itself beyond all being and, as Plotinus often insists, beyond all real knowledge. So the intelligible essence (the second hypostasis, intermediate between the One and soul) may be thought of as an unmoving circle which has the One or the Good as its center,[8] and it is this proximity to the very source of all unity that gives to the intelligible essence the kind of life that we call eternity.

We should be careful, continues Plotinus, not to be misled by the word "always," which we may use for the sake of clarity. When we apply it to that being which is eternal, we should not allow it to bring in the idea of extension. It

[7] 37d.
[8] Cf. iv. 4. 16.

might be better to speak of "being" only, without employing any attribute. But "being" has sometimes been used to designate substance, and some have thought that there is substance even in the realm of becoming. To convey our meaning more properly, therefore, we speak of being that is always. It is true being, a power that has no extension and lacks nothing.[9]

Everything which is in time, even when it seems complete, still has need of a future (6. 38); it is, therefore, deficient to the extent that it is in need of time. But we are seeking a being that has no need whatsoever of a future, one that is ever complete, one whose being does not come from anything quantitative, but is prior to all quantity. Since it is not quantitative, it must have no contact with quantity; its life, like its essence, must be without parts. When Plato says of the craftsman, "He was good," [10] he does not mean to give the craftsman a temporal attribute, or to indicate that the universe had a temporal beginning. Rather the craftsman is given the priority of cause. The expression is used only for the sake of the demonstration, and Plato corrects himself later, indicating that such an expression is not properly applied to beings that partake of eternity.

### APPROACH TO THE PROBLEM OF TIME

Thus we conclude the discussion of eternity that is necessary for the understanding of time in Plotinus. The transition from eternity to time is made very neatly (7. 1). In speaking of eternity, asks Plotinus, are we not discoursing

---

[9] There is an illuminating note on this passage by Helene Weiss, "An Interpretative Note on a Passage in Plotinus' *On Eternity and Time* (III. 7. 6)," *Classical Philology*, XXXVI (1941), 230–239. There may be some question as to the precise interpretation of ll. 23–24.

[10] *Timaeus* 29e; but cf. *ibid.* 37e–38a.

about things that are foreign to us, bearing witness, as it were, for utter strangers? Since it is impossible to have an understanding of something with which we have no contact, it must be that we are partakers somehow in eternity. But how can this be true of beings that exist in time? Perhaps we can see how it is possible to be in time and in eternity if first we find out what time is. Consequently we must descend from eternity to the lower stage of time. Our path has been upward thus far; now we must descend, not too far, but only so far as time descended from eternity.

Plotinus thus indicates that in the subsequent discussion of time we shall be able to understand time only as something following upon eternity. Though we are not yet told what the relation of the two is, we know from the general trend of the philosophy of Plotinus that in all probability we have here a series, as with other emanations from the primal One, with a diminishing power at each successive stage. No one stage can be understood except in relation to the others in the series, though of course this is not a temporal series, since every stage in it has always existed. Plotinus has indicated, therefore, that just as the sensible world cannot be understood apart from the intelligible world, which is its counterpart in the realm of true being, so time, which clearly pertains to the sensible world, must be set in relation to eternity, which we have seen is an effulgence proceeding from the intelligible world, in fact, its very life. It is possible, as Plotinus has indicated, to begin with time and go upward to eternity by reminiscence. But this would be only a pathway into the intelligible world, and we should still be obliged to carry out the same examination of that world as we have done thus far to determine the exact nature of eternity. Such a pathway is at this point unnecessary for Plotinus, since the whole background of this treatise supplies an intimate knowledge of the intelligible world. We have only to take our previously acquired data and determine clearly one phase of intelligible existence.[11] A knowledge of time aids us in our search for eternity only in supplying the rudimentary means of which the novice would have to avail himself. But a knowledge of eternity is no such incidental means to an understanding of time. For time in its entire reality is dependent on whatever members of the series are prior to it. Any knowledge we obtain, therefore, of the essential nature of time will come from finding its proper position in the series, especially its relation to eternity, with which it is generally contrasted.[12]

Plotinus now indicates the method he will pursue in the investigation of time (7. 10). Suppose our predecessors had said nothing about time. In that case we should be obliged to speak of eternity and then join to it the next in the series, namely, time. In giving our opinions about time in this manner, we should try to reconcile them with the general idea of time that all of us already possess. But as it is we shall first be obliged to investigate the doctrines concerning time handed down by the ancients, at least those doctrines most worthy of consideration, and see whether our mode of procedure accords with any of these views.

Thus Plotinus indicates a twofold source of our knowl-

---

[11] The three treatises on the categories of being (vi. 1–3), important in the investigation of eternity, were written, according to the indications of Porphyry (*Life of Plotinus*, chap. 5), just before this treatise.

[12] In the thought of Plotinus (e.g., ii. 4. 3–5) each stage of the emanations is said to be matter with reference to the one immediately preceding it, and is determined to its mode of being by that predecessor. Thus throughout the series, however far it progresses, there is the connecting link of analogy or proportion. Each stage is a mean between its predecessor and its successor. Guitton, *op. cit.*, pp. 85–90, has some interesting remarks on causality by inversion.

edge of time. In the first place, everyone knows something about time, whatever his philosophical method or lack of it, through observation and introspection. And everyone thinks that he knows what time is, at least until he tries to give an explanation of it. This common knowledge of time is something that we must consider, and any detailed examination of time must not be out of harmony with it. Otherwise we should be explaining something other than that which men in general call time. This conviction of men must be a common ground of all philosophical explanations. The divergence of belief is only in the explanation of what this generally known thing, time, is in its essential nature. The second source of knowledge is a philosophical investigation carried on according to a definite method. And Plotinus clearly sets forth the method he is going to pursue, the linking of time to its natural predecessor, eternity. The results of this investigation we should expect to be in harmony with time as it is generally recognized by men. But there is something else which we should do first of all. We must see whether our predecessors have investigated the problem in a way that we might find satisfactory. The results that they have attained may be an adequate solution of the problem, or, if not, they must be shown inadequate, and the proper solution must take account of these inadequacies.

Plotinus now divides the various doctrines about time in a threefold manner (7. 17). Time has been identified with motion, with the moving object, or with some attribute of motion. It is contrary to the general idea of time to say that it is rest, the object at rest, or some attribute of rest. Of those who say that time is identical with motion, some think of motion as a whole, others that of the universe. Those who consider time the moving object say that it is the sphere of the universe. Those who think time some attribute of motion call it an extension of motion, or a measure, or in general an accompaniment of motion; and these speak either of motion as a whole or of regular motion only.

### THE TWO VIEWS THAT TIME IS MOTION AND THE SPHERE OF THE UNIVERSE

Having classified the various views of time in a way that seems to be exhaustive, Plotinus proceeds to examine them (8. 1). Time cannot be motion, whether we take all motions and consider them as having a kind of unity as motions or take regular motion only. For in either case the motion is in time and is by that very fact something different from time. If there is some motion that is not in time, then it is even farther from being time. This general consideration Plotinus makes more specific by saying that motion can cease and be intermittent, but time cannot. There is an exception to this statement, however, namely, the motion of the universe. But this revolution is completed in a certain time which is different from the time in which half a revolution is accomplished. Thus the revolution is in two different times, in accordance with the amount of it that we take. There is a second argument to show that the motion of the universe is in time. We say that the motion of the outermost sphere is the fastest. This indicates that the motion and time are different, for the swiftest motion traverses a greater distance than all the others in a lesser time. Our conclusion must be that all motion, even that of the universe, is in time and therefore different from time.

It is interesting to note Plotinus' procedure in criticizing this first view of time, especially in comparison with that of Aristotle, who also investigates the proposal that time is motion. First of all, we are given no hint of what Plotinus himself considers time to be, no reference of time to eternity, which Plotinus has indicated is necessary to a full understanding of time. It is not necessary as yet to bring in eternity and show the true nature of time. Plotinus is here a simple analyst, much like Aristotle. It requires a very brief consideration to show that the view that time is motion is not in accord with the general belief in time, since the accepted idea of time implies that time is different from motion, that motion is in time in the various ways that Plotinus sets forth. The discussion thus far is therefore on the same level as Aristotle's dialectic. We shall expect to see it rise as we proceed.

But there are likewise differences in Plotinus that are not unimportant. In the details of the argumentation there is, to be sure, much similarity between Plotinus and Aristotle. The statement that all motion is in time is reminiscent of Aristotle's teaching that all things moving and at rest are in time.[13] Plotinus says that motion may be intermittent, but not time, though the motion of the universe is not intermittent. So Aristotle admits that an individual motion may lapse, but time will never fail, because it is always at a beginning in the now; and the heaven is always in motion.[14] Moreover, Aristotle is in agreement with Plotinus in saying that the revolution of the heaven is not time, and that motion cannot be time because motion is faster and slower, but time is not.[15]

Plotinus, however, has infused into these points a new spirit. It is only after a lengthy discussion that Aristotle speaks of moving things and things at rest being in time.

[13] *Physics* 221b7–23.
[14] *Ibid.* 220a7–8, 222b6–7, 260a14–19; *On the Heaven* 279b1–3.
[15] *Physics* 218b1–5, 13–18.

But Plotinus, profiting by Aristotle's labors, can state this without any preliminaries and base his entire distinction between time and motion on the consideration that all motion is in time, and if any motion is not in time, it is even farther from being time. This appears to involve a difficulty for Plotinus if we look forward to his later doctrine that time is a kind of motion, namely, that it is the life of soul; this is a motion that is not in time, but is time. But at this stage Plotinus is justified in denying that time is motion, because he has restricted the discussion to those motions, such as the motion of the universe, which the philosophers whom he is criticizing had in mind. Moreover, Plotinus believes that moving things in general are seen to be in time because the motion lapses but time does not.

Aristotle rather tends to say that, since motion is in time as in its number, the lapses of motion, that is, periods of rest, are likewise in time, since rest is the privation of motion.[16] His own procedure thus forces Plotinus to give especial attention to the motion of the heavens, which does not lapse. It is shown to be in time, and therefore different from time, while Aristotle says merely that the revolution is not time, because a part of the revolution is a kind of time but is not a revolution. Likewise, Plotinus uses the relative speed of the spheres to show that they are in time, while Aristotle says that motion is not time because motion as faster and slower is determined by time. This difference of emphasis involves a compression that is possible for Plotinus only because Aristotle's finished work lay before him. Since Aristotle has set forth a plausible meaning of existence in time, Plotinus can use it in his dialectical discussion, though Aristotle himself was not able to do this.

[16] *Ibid.* 221b7–23.

This raises the question how far Plotinus must accept the definition of time given by Aristotle, on which the significance of existence in time is based. Our answer must be that at this point Aristotle's definition of time is satisfactory to Plotinus. On this level he can admit that time is used by men to measure motion, though this may not be a complete explanation of time on a higher level.

There is one further difference between Plotinus and Aristotle, that is, the order of the various details. Aristotle in his dialectical argument first denies that time is the motion of the universe, then that it is the sphere itself, finally that it is motion of any kind. Plotinus begins by denying that time is motion in general or any regular motion, which includes implicitly the motion of the universe. Motion in general is open to the objection that it can lapse, but the motion of the universe must be shown to be in time in another way, and this introduces two arguments, namely, that a part of the revolution takes place in a lesser time than a complete revolution, and that to say that the outermost sphere is the fastest is to admit that the heavenly spheres are in time. Aristotle's approach, as we saw, was to attach time to motion as its number, not any one kind of motion, but motion as such. The fact that some men think that time is the motion of the universe only shows that there is thought to be some connection between time and motion. But at a later stage in his argument Aristotle comes to the consideration that time has an especially close connection with the motion of the heavens. In Plotinus we again have a compression. He has no desire to show that time as employed by the physicist is attached to motion as such and then by a lengthy discussion trace all motion and consequently all time to the heavens. Looking at the two kinds of motion at once, he sees that the motion of the heavens

offers a better explanation of the uniformity of time, and
for that reason demands special consideration.

He now treats the second view of time, that it is the
sphere itself (8. 20). This can hardly be true if time is not
the motion of the sphere, since it was thought to be the
sphere on account of the motion. This criticism is as summary as Aristotle's, but offers a different reason for the doctrine criticized.[17]

### THE STOIC VIEW THAT TIME IS AN EXTENSION OF MOTION

Plotinus proceeds to the third possibility, that time is
some attribute of motion, and, first of all, an extension of
motion (8. 23). Here again we have the distinction between motion in general and the motion of the universe,
and the latter, being more plausible, is criticized in the second place and at greater length. First, time cannot be an
extension of motion in general, because all motions do not
have the same extension, even those of the same kind. Thus
local motion is faster and slower. And the two different
extensions would be measured by some other thing which
would more rightly be called time. If time were an extension of motion, then there would be an infinite number of
times.

If time is not the extension of motion in general, but only
of regular motion, still this cannot be all regular motion,
for these many regular motions would give us many times
at once. So we must consider time to be the extension of
the motion of the universe. But suppose that this is an extension in the motion itself; how would it differ from the
motion? It might be motion considered as having a definite
quantity. But if this quantity of motion is measured by the
space that the motion has traversed, and this is the exten-

[17] *Ibid.* 218b5–9.

sion proposed, this is not time but space. But suppose that
the motion has an extension that is due to its own continuity,
and to the fact that it does not cease, but goes on and on.
This would be nothing more, however, than the quantity
or amount of the motion itself. This is no more time than
would be a certain quantity or intensity of heat. There is
only motion occurring over and over again, as in flowing
water, and the extension to be observed therein. The fact
that the motion occurs over and over again can give us a
number, like two or three, and the extension that is observed will be a matter of quantity or bulk.[18] We are thus
presented with a plurality in motion that will give us either
a mere abstract number or an extension manifested in what
we might call the bulk of the motion, which will not have
in it the idea of time, but will be only a definite quantity
of motion taking place in time. If someone should insist
that this quantity of motion is time, then time will not be
everywhere, but will have motion as its substrate in such a
way as to lead us back again to the doctrine that time is
identical with motion. For such an extension is not outside
of the motion but is identical with motion insofar as this is
not instantaneous. But that which is not instantaneous must
be in time. Thus, he concludes, both motion possessing
extension and the extension of motion are not themselves
time; rather they are in time.

We have thus considered the possibility that time is the
extension of the motion itself, and seen that this must give

---

[18] Guitton, *op. cit.*, p. 11, n. 1, following the translation of Bréhier,
wrongly takes this extension as one of space, though we have clearly discussed the extension of space previously. Plotinus is thinking here of a
quantity of motion similar to a quantity of heat, apart from the space
traversed by the motion. Bréhier and Guitton are reading into Plotinus
Aristotle's doctrine that the amount of motion depends upon the length
of the space traversed.

us a quantitative idea of the motion that may lead to space, which is not time; or to the plurality of an abstract number, which is not time either; or to a definite bulk of motion, which again is not time, but is in time. To say that the motion has a certain extension in its bulk is not to make this extension time; it is simply to recognize that the motion is not instantaneous, but is in time, which is something different from the motion. Thus this view is only another way of saying that time is motion, and Plotinus criticizes it in the same way.

But suppose now that the extension in question is not one that belongs to the motion itself, but is one that gives dimension to the motion because the motion keeps pace, as it were, with it (8. 53). But what this thing is with which motion keeps pace we are not told. Time is clearly that in which motion takes place, but time is what we have been seeking from the beginning to define. If one were asked to define time, he surely would not call it an extension of motion in time. What, then, is this extension called time, which is outside of the extension of motion itself? On the other hand, if time is an extension of motion itself we think of another objection (which really results from the fact that time thus considered is not everywhere, as Plotinus has stated earlier). Where shall we put the extension of rest? For one thing can be at rest just as long as another is in motion, and we should say that the time is the same for both, and therefore distinct from them. What, then, is this extension that we are seeking? It obviously cannot be spatial, though space is something likewise distinct from motion and rest.

Thus Plotinus shows at some length that time is not to be defined as an extension of motion. The dialectic is on the same level for the most part as in the criticism of the view that time is identical with motion. For the idea of extension carried in one direction may be reduced to the same doctrine. Moreover, it is easy to see that time is not space, though space is a kind of extension connected with motion. But there are two interesting considerations in view of what is coming shortly. Plotinus will not tolerate the identification of time with an abstract number; this is important in his examination of Aristotle. And he will not permit any explanation that does not tell what time is in its very essence. It is not sufficient to say that it is an extension that gives dimension to motion. This may be true, but it is not telling us what this thing is. Thus Plotinus dismisses the view of time that has traditionally been ascribed to the Stoic philosophers.

### THE ARISTOTELIAN VIEW THAT TIME IS THE NUMBER OR MEASURE OF MOTION

Plotinus now proceeds to consider whether time is the number or measure of motion, the definition of Aristotle (9. 1). Measure is a better term, he says, since motion is continuous; but throughout the passage he employs both terms, not always with careful distinction, speaking even of number as measuring. If we consider motion as a whole, we have the same difficulty as previously. How can one number irregular and nonuniform motion? What number or measure will there be, or what will be the standard of measurement? If time is the number or measure of every sort of motion, that would be like the number ten measuring horses and oxen, or the same measure for liquids and solids. This tells us what time measures, namely, motions; but it does not yet tell us what time is. The number ten can be known apart from the horses it measures, and any measure has a certain nature as measure, even if it has never measured. So we should be able to say what time is in its essential nature as a measure. If time is only a number, then how does it differ from an abstract number, such as ten? If, on the other hand, it is a continuous measure, it will have some quantity, like a cubit-rule. It will therefore be a magnitude, just like a line keeping pace with motion. But how will it measure the motion with which it is keeping pace? Why should one of the two be the measure rather than the other?

In criticizing the Aristotelian definition of time, Plotinus has first made the distinction between motion in general and regular motion, the same distinction, he tells us, that was previously made in the discussion of time as the extension of motion. The first question he asks introduces us to the many difficulties he sees in the treatment of time by Aristotle. What measure or standard of measure can the motion of itself offer if the motion possesses no uniformity or regularity? Aristotle, as we saw, found this no difficulty. Men are able to measure motion of any kind by means of time, and the irregularity of motion only serves to show that motion and time are different. But for Plotinus this is a statement of fact without any explanation of the nature of time in itself to illuminate it. We must show that time has some kind of independent existence apart from motion even before it measures motion, if we expect to understand how time measures all motion. Consequently, if time is said to measure all kinds of motion, we are led to wonder what sort of thing it can be in itself.

Plotinus suggests that it could be like the number ten, which measures different things, or some kind of measure that has various capacities. But how does this help us, he asks, toward an understanding of time? On the one hand, to define time as the measure of motion is to tell us what time measures, not what time itself is. The number and measure already mentioned can be known apart from the things they measure. But we cannot, on the other hand, call time an abstract number, because that would give us no right to call it alone of all numbers time; nor can we make it a continuous measure keeping pace with motion as a line might do, because this unbroken continuum surely would have no more right to measure the motion than to be measured by the motion. For if it keeps pace with the motion, it will have no differentiation within itself whereby to measure the motion.

Moreover, continues Plotinus, it would be better to consider this magnitude accompanying motion not in connection with motion in general, but with that particular motion with which it is keeping pace (9. 22). This motion will have to be continuous and uniform; in fact, it will have to be a single motion, that of the universe.[19] Such a motion, Plotinus thinks, is necessary to account for the continuity and other characteristics of time, which presumably has its existence only by keeping pace with the motion it measures. Thus, he indicates, if we are to make time a measure of motion and at the same time preserve the unity and continuity that we realize it possesses, we cannot think of it as the measure of all motion but only of a single, uniform motion, specifically that of the universe.

There is not a complete disagreement on this point between Plotinus and Aristotle. Aristotle would admit that there is an intimate relation between time and the motion of the universe, so that time might be called in one sense the measure of the motion of the universe. But Aristotle's understanding of this statement would be conditioned by his method of leading up to it. His analysis shows first of

[19] Cf. 9. 32-35.

all that time is the measure of motion of any kind whatsoever, because all motion is in time and is measured by time.
But since all motion is measured by regular circular motion,
we may say that time is the measure of circular motion and
is measured by this kind of motion.[20] It is only in contexts
far removed from these that time is related to the motion of
the universe, because all motion can be traced back to the
motion of the outermost sphere of the universe, and it is
this continuous motion that makes time continuous.[21] Thus
it is not until we arrive at the motion of the universe that
we have the ultimate cause of time's continuity. But long
before that we can show that time is the measure of circular
motion, because only this motion can be continuous and
eternal, and before this we can so analyze time that it may
be called simply the measure of motion, and a continuous
measure, as analysis will show.

Plotinus, however, not having this analytic approach of
Aristotle, brings in another compression of the long and
deliberate Aristotelian argument. Time must be the measure — if a measure at all — of a single motion, that of the
universe, for time is continuous. This observation of
Plotinus supplements his criticism, at the beginning of this
chapter, of the view that time is the measure of all motion.
In that case he was inquiring, from the standpoint of the
motion, how irregular motion is susceptible to measure
(unless we introduce some external number or measure
that the definition does not specify). Here he insists that if
time is to be continuous, as we all admit, it must be the
measure of one motion, that of the universe. But he has
already shown that if time is made continuous by being the
measure of motion, keeping pace with the motion, it is hard

[20] *Physics* 223a29–224a2.
[21] *On the Heaven* 283b26–284a11.

to see why one should be the measure any more than the other.

After showing that it is difficult to maintain that time has some reality as a number, or as a continuous measure apart from motion, depending on the motion, however, for its continuity, Plotinus proceeds to examine the possibility that this thing that measures motion is not to be considered apart from the motion but only (as Aristotle might have said) along with the measured motion (9. 24). If this is our position, then clearly motion will be that which is measured, and some kind of magnitude again will do the measuring. Since the two of these do not exist apart from each other — the measured motion and the measuring magnitude — we may well ask the question which one will be time. Time will be either the motion considered as measured by the magnitude, or the magnitude that measures, or possibly a third thing that uses the magnitude, as it might a cubit-rule, in order to measure the quantity of the motion.

Here again Plotinus suggests that such a view would be easier to maintain if we were speaking of a single, uniform motion, such as that of the universe. From his point of view the uniformity of the motion would be even more important here than previously, where time was considered as something having its own reality apart from the motion. If in that case the motion had to be uniform in order to secure the uniformity of time, Plotinus would doubtless consider the uniformity of the motion more clearly desirable for a view that states that time has no reality apart from the measured motion.

If, then, continues Plotinus, we consider the measured motion as being in some way time, that is, motion measured by some quantity or other, we should keep in mind that we are not allowing the motion to measure itself, but are introducing a continuous measure to measure it (a measure that differs from the motion in aspect or definition, as Aristotle would consider it, if not in substrate) (9. 35). But then we are obliged to look for some kind of measure for this magnitude, in order that the motion may be measured by a measure that has in itself a certain quantity.

Thus in the measured motion the magnitude that keeps pace with the motion and measures it has, Plotinus suggests, no more right to be called time, as a measure, than the motion itself, because this magnitude also needs something else as measure to give it a definite quantity. In this way Plotinus indicates that if time is to be accepted as the continuous thing that we believe it is, it will be incapable of measuring anything unless something else has previously imposed a measure upon it and divided its unbroken continuity. This is true if time has its own reality apart from the motion, as we saw previously, and it is true here, where time is considered as having its reality not as separate from the measured motion, but as distinct only in definition.

If the magnitude that keeps pace with the motion demands some third thing to give it a definite quantity, this will be some kind of number, and, if we think of time as being a measure of motion, this number will more properly be called time than the magnitude itself, since it is the ultimate measure of the magnitude and the motion (9. 43). But can we think of any such number other than abstract number composed of units? It is difficult to see how this abstract number will do any measuring, this number which would presumably use the continuous magnitude in order to measure the motion. This number, therefore, would be an example of the third possibility that Plotinus has suggested in addition to the measured motion and the magnitude that measures it, namely, that which uses the magnitude to measure the motion. But now Plotinus wonders how this abstract number can measure the continuous magnitude that is keeping pace with the motion in order to divide it into units of measure by which motion can be measured. For example, how could the number three divide this continuous magnitude so as to give us three units of measure for motion, such as three days or three years (which periods would not deserve to be called time so much as the abstract number that provided the ultimate measure)?

But even if we should discover, continues Plotinus, how this abstract number could measure, we should not thus discover time measuring, but only a certain amount of time, which is something different from time (9. 46). That is to say, Plotinus cannot accept time as being identical with abstract number, although the view that time is the measure of motion would seem logically to reduce time to this. But even if we were to grant that an abstract number could measure a continuous quantity, we must realize that we have here only a certain quantity of time, that is, a certain number of units of time, but we have not been told what it is of which we use a given number of units for purposes of measuring. This difficulty arises from offering, as if it could be the essence of time, a mere function, that of providing a quantitative measure. This is surely the fundamental criticism that Plotinus offers of the Aristotelian approach to time; before we consider what a certain amount of time is, we should be able to indicate what time is in itself, and it is his conviction that he will be able to discover what it is before taking certain amounts of it.

Someone might now suggest that time is a number that measures motion from without in the same way as the number ten measures horses, but has its own reality apart from

the horses (9. 51). The statement of Aristotle,[22] intended
to show the similarity between time and abstract number,
Plotinus is unwilling to accept because again it does not tell
us what time is in itself before it measures, in the same way
as we can tell what the number ten is in its own proper
nature.

Plotinus now proceeds to take up another aspect of Aristotle's definition of time: that which accompanying motion
measures it according to prior and posterior (9. 55). His
first criticism is that we do not yet know clearly what this
thing is that measures according to prior and posterior.
(We shall see more and more evidence that for Plotinus
Aristotle's approach, restricted as it is to a consideration of
what time means for the physical philosopher who studies
motion, does not go far enough.) But, he continues, finding
a further objection, that which measures according to prior
and posterior will have to measure according to time,
whether it uses a point of time or something else by which
to measure according to prior and posterior. Therefore,
this thing that measures motion by prior and posterior must
in some way be attached to time and in contact with it in
order to measure. For the prior and posterior is itself something temporal, unless it refers to place.

Aristotle's view that the prior and posterior is first of all
in place and then in the motion as passing from one place to
another, and that time numbers according to a prior and
posterior that is fundamentally spatial, not temporal — all
this Plotinus does not consider explicitly. He does suggest
that there is a spatial prior and posterior, but he seems to
consider it irrelevant, and we can imagine why. Aristotle
would say that the student of nature receives his idea of time
from numbering motion as it passes from place to place. But

22 *Physics* 220a23–26.

Plotinus would wonder how a numbering process that is based on mere spatial difference could give us anything more than a quantity of space. Moreover, he believes, as we shall see, that motion passes from place to place only because it is in time already, and therefore the temporal prior and posterior is more fundamental than the spatial, not the reverse. In fact, he would probably ask how we could call one place prior and another posterior rather than only different unless time had somehow entered into our calculations.

The prior, therefore, he continues (9. 64), is time that ends at the present moment, while the posterior is time that begins from the present moment. Since the number that measures motion, whether motion in general or regular motion, according to prior and posterior is thus measuring according to time, we must conclude that this number is different from time, and we have not yet arrived at the nature of time.

Further, Plotinus now asks, why should time begin to exist only through the intervention of number (9. 68)? It makes no difference, Plotinus adds parenthetically, whether the number be considered as measured or as measuring, since the same number may be either one or the other.[23] (Aristotle had called time a number that is numbered, not numbering.[24] It is like ten horses, which are numbered, rather than the abstract number ten, which numbers. Although Aristotle and Plotinus differ on the nature of number, Aristotle would agree that a quantity of time, which is numbered in the motion, has a corresponding numbering number, just as the ten horses have. Plotinus, at any rate, objects to considering time as essentially quantitative in any re-

[23] Cf. vi. 6. 15.
[24] *Physics* 219b7–8.

spect.) Why should not time exist without the intervention
of number if motion exists with the prior and posterior in it
already? The view that number must intervene would be
like saying that a magnitude has not its own quantity unless
someone measures this quantity.

Aristotle admits that, in a sense, motion has the prior and
posterior that provides the substrate of time, but time itself
demands that this prior and posterior be numbered by the
mind.[25] He would doubtless reply to Plotinus by saying
that we can think of a temporal prior and posterior as existing in motion only because in so doing our mind has numbered two different phases of the motion. Therefore, time
is that aspect of the motion by which it is numbered. But
Plotinus would ask, as we have seen somewhat earlier, how
a mere quantity of motion could give us the idea of time any
more than a quantity of something else, such as heat. Consequently, there must be something temporal in motion independent of the mind that measures the motion. We must
find what time is, therefore, apart from a measuring of motion or especially of time itself. Again Plotinus is dissatisfied
with the method of Aristotle; if time is only a number, how
does it differ from abstract number, and if it is more than an
abstract number, but may be reckoned in terms of it, what
is the thing that is so reckoned?

Moreover, since time is infinite and is admitted to be so,[26]
Plotinus wonders how we can speak of number with respect
to it (9. 75). We might take a part of time and measure it
by means of a number, but this would mean that time would
exist in itself even before it was thus measured.

Aristotle would say that time is infinite, and number
also, in the same way as certain other things are infinite,

[25] *Ibid.* 223a25–29.
[26] Also by Aristotle, e.g., *ibid.* 267b25.

whenever one thing, such as one number, can be taken after another with a new one always available.[27] Thus time, being a kind of number, is potentially infinite. But, Plotinus would say, time, in whatever way it is infinite, cannot be used to measure motion if it is taken as an infinite quantity. If we were to use it as a measure at all, we should have to take a portion of it, such as three days or three years; and thus to make it available as a measure time itself would have to receive some kind of finite number. But we have not yet answered what it is that receives a number, what this thing is that we divide into three days or three years in order to use it as a measure.

Plotinus now criticizes another point in Aristotle's treatment of time (9. 78). He asks why time should not exist before the soul that measures exists. This would be true in a way if we could say that time somehow receives its origin from soul (as Plotinus himself will say later), but even so it is not through the process of measuring that time is brought into existence, for time exists in its own proper quantity even if there is no measuring at all, whether of motion or of time itself. Plotinus now returns to the threefold suggestion he made about time if it is to be considered along with the measured motion; that is, time will be either the measured motion, or the magnitude that measures it, or a third thing using the magnitude as it would a cubit-rule in order to measure the motion. Someone might say that the soul is this thing that uses the magnitude in order to measure and is therefore time. But to say that the soul considered as measuring motion *is* time, how does this fit in with our common conception of time? [28]

---

[27] *Ibid.* 206a25–207b15.
[28] Plotinus speaks occasionally elsewhere about the Aristotelian definition of time. An especially pertinent passage is vi. 1. 5, where Plotinus

In a brief chapter of transition (10) Plotinus, for the sake of completeness, parenthetically remarks that if anyone were to say that time is the measure of the motion of the universe, the same arguments, generally speaking, could be used against him as have been used in criticizing the statement that time is the measure of motion in general, since we should have to leave out of our discussion only the irregularity that motion in general possesses (10. 12). We will recall that Plotinus directed his arguments for the most part against the view that time is the measure of motion in such a way as to indicate that this view would be better if it referred only to the regular motion of the universe, but that in any case it was untenable.

### THE VIEW THAT TIME IS AN ACCOMPANIMENT OF MOTION

We have still to consider the possibility that time is the accompaniment of motion (10. 1). We cannot very well, says Plotinus, appreciate the significance of this proposal before the one who advances it tells us what the thing is that is accompanying motion. This thing might perhaps be

indicates that various things that are considered to be quantities are in themselves really not quantities. So Plotinus thinks that time is not in itself a quantity. For if we consider time as that which measures, then we must think, looking again for the thing that does the measuring, that it is either soul or the now. If we consider time quantitative, however, as something that is measured, then it will be quantitative by having a certain length, such as that of a year; but insofar as it is time, it will have some nature that is different from quantity. Time is not a quantity; quantity which is not attached to something else but exists in itself is quantity in the true sense. If we should call everything that participates in quantity a quantity, then we should be obliged to call even substance quantity. Plotinus thus rejects the possibility that either soul or the now is time, since presumably they do not conform to our idea of time. On the other hand, he thinks that we must look beyond the quantitative aspect of time to the nature of time in itself. This is in conformity with Plotinus' whole treatment of quantity and his disagreement with Aristotle's discussion of this category.

time. Again Plotinus is not satisfied with a statement that
offers a superficial description of what time does; he wants
to know what time is. But he offers another criticism as
well. If there is any such accompaniment of motion, then
we must ask whether it is posterior to motion, simultaneous
with it, or prior to it. Whichever of these is the case, the
accompaniment will be in time. (For these expressions all
conform to the general conception of time, and in fact
Plotinus in the preceding chapter pointed out the temporal
nature of prior and posterior.) If time is this accompaniment, then time will be an accompaniment of motion in time.
The Stoic Chrysippus may be the object of this criticism.

If the one who suggested this definition of time were to
object to Plotinus' criticism as unfair, Plotinus would doubtless say that the other had been too careless in offering a
supposed definition without telling what time really is, and
therefore deserved this criticism. Moreover, Plotinus thinks
that time and motion are too intimately connected in their
very nature to permit the use of the term "accompaniment,"
which suggests something rather incidental to motion.
Something so incidental to motion clearly will not be time,
but will be in time. There is no need for Plotinus to make a
distinction here between motion in general and regular motion, because the term "accompaniment" is inadequate in
either case for the reasons that he has given.

The various explanations of time that have been offered
by our many predecessors, continues Plotinus, have been set
forth so fully that to attempt a detailed account would involve us in a long historical discussion (10. 9). We have
said enough in passing about these explanations (without
giving Plato's, however), and besides we are seeking what
time is, not what it is not. Therefore, it is now our task to
tell what the nature of time is.

### THE DERIVATION OF TIME FROM ETERNITY

We must go back, Plotinus says, to that state which we called eternity, that life unchanging, ever complete, infinite, absolutely fixed, reposing in the One, and directed towards it (11. 1). Time was not as yet, or at least it was not for those beings in the realm of intellect. Time was destined to come into existence in the sense that in definition and nature it belongs to a later stage of existence.

Thus Plotinus is carrying out his purpose of deriving time from eternity, which is following the order of the things themselves. There is no time in the world of intellect, for intellect, the second Plotinian hypostasis, is fixed and unchanging in its turning toward the primal One, which is beyond all being and the source of all being. Time comes later, but we should not think that it has a first moment of its existence, for it is later only in the sense that it belongs to a grade of existence that is inferior to and dependent on intelligible being. Just as this later existence is dependent on the earlier, so time, we shall see, depends on eternity.

Since the intelligible beings repose in complete tranquillity (11. 6), we must ask how time first descended from them (though, of course, the descent did not have a first moment, but is something that is ever taking place). Since the Muses did not as yet exist, we cannot call upon them in the fashion of the poet, but perhaps we can ask time itself to tell us the story of its coming to birth. It would doubtless make some such answer as this: Earlier, before time itself generated this "earlier" and, being bound up with it, began to strive for the "later," it reposed in the realm of being, but was not time, for it too was perfectly tranquil in being. But there was a nature that was eager for action, desirous of ruling and possessing itself, and anxious to seek more than it possessed already. This nature, therefore, began to move, and time itself began to move. As the two moved ever and ever to what lay before them, to a later stage that was not the same but always different, and created a line of progress, as it were, time was fashioned as the image of eternity. For there was a certain power of soul that was not tranquil but, desiring always to transfer what it saw in the realm of intellect to another state of existence, was unwilling to have its full possession completely present to it at once. So, to take an analogy, from the seed that is at rest the creative power unwinding itself outwards progresses toward plurality, manifesting the plurality by division; in giving up its unity by no longer containing itself and in spending its unity elsewhere, it advances toward a weaker extension of itself.

In the same manner soul, in making the universe an imitation of intelligible being, the sensible universe that has a motion which is not that of intelligible being but is like it and strives to be an image of it, first of all made itself temporal instead of eternal, and then made the created universe the servant of time by making it to be entirely in time and comprehending all its development within time. Just as the sensible universe moves in soul (for it has no other place than soul), so it received its motion within the time of soul. Soul, in which the universe moves, produces its acts one after another in constant succession, and it is along with this activity that soul generated succession. With every new thought that follows its predecessor there comes into existence that which formerly was not, since the thought itself had not previously been actualized and the life that is now differs from that which preceded it. This life of soul, therefore, together with being different and because of this difference possessed different time. This extension of its life

possessed time; the constant progress of this life has time
ever anew; and the life which has passed by has past time.
It would seem, therefore, that time is the life of soul as it
passes from one stage of actualization to another.

It might be well at this point to say that when Plotinus
speaks of the productive activity of soul as if it had a succession of thoughts whose progressive actualization brings
about the sensible universe with its manifold changes, and
in particular the circular motion of the heaven, he is not to
be understood as saying strictly that in the life of soul as
such there is succession. Rather there is succession only in
the products of soul. The nature of soul as such is eternal
and is not in time, although soul generates time in which
the products of soul's activity have their prior and posterior.
But this succession of prior and posterior is not in the soul
itself, for soul contains the principles of all things without
any difference of time or place. When through the activity
of soul sensible things come into existence they cannot exist
at the same time any more than they can in the same place.[29]

We should not think, however, in view of Plotinus' philosophy as a whole, that time is the prior and posterior in
the motion of the universe any more than that it is the life
of soul as such. Time is the life of soul, not in itself, but
only considered insofar as it is the principle of life and motion for the universe. Time hovers, as it were, between soul
and the universe, and it has in it prior and posterior only in
the sense that the life communicated by soul to the sensible
world is received continuously by this lower world and
translated into motion, the best manifestation of this continuous communication of life being the uniform motion of
the heaven. Thus it is very important for Plotinus to affirm

[29] iv. 4. 15–16. This interesting juxtaposition of time and place is not
amplified.

with Plato that time came into existence along with the universe, as he will do shortly, for unless there were a universe motivated by soul there would be no way in which we could speak of soul's continuity as a principle of life, since this activity of soul may be said to have prior and posterior in it only from the standpoint of the universe. When, therefore, Plotinus applies to the soul and its life terms that seem to make it extended, we should remember that soul is an extension that is inextended.[30]

### PLOTINUS AND PLATO

It should now be noted how Plotinus adapts Plato's statements about time to his own purposes. This will be seen in greater detail as his explanation of time and soul continues, but it might be well to look now at the direction his argument has taken thus far. Plato says that time is the image of eternity, and explains this metaphor by indicating that time and eternity are in the same proportion as number and unity, since number can be considered as generated by unity and a product of it. Moreover, the number series that time represents is without end, just as eternity is always. This is the significance for Plato, therefore, of calling time the image and eternity the model.

Plotinus will also call time an image of eternity, but in the light of what he has already said we can expect this to have a much different meaning. First of all, there is no reference whatsoever to time as a number, and even when Plotinus recalls phrases from the *Timaeus* he does not mention anything Plato says of the numbers of time. The reason in part is that Plotinus has elevated unity to a position above eternity, and number in his system is raised to the level of in-

[30] Cf. iv. 4. 16.

tellect and the ideas, that is, to eternity itself. In this way he tends to limit himself to the ideal numbers,[31] and number must henceforth have for him less flexibility than it has for Plato, who can also speak of the numbers of time. This emphasis on the ideal numbers prevents Plotinus from using number with the wider range that many of his terms, such as motion and life, possess. It is, in general, limited to one level of the Plotinian dialectic by becoming closely identified with intellect, which is one of the fixed points in the dialectic.

Instead of the proportion involving one and number Plotinus introduces a discussion centered about the concept of life. This comes about because, just as unity has been placed by Plotinus above intellect, so an intermediary is introduced between eternity and time, namely, soul. It could not be otherwise for Plotinus since soul is another fixed point that must, in the order of nature, precede the sensible universe. Soul must precede time because we understand time to be related somehow to the motion of a universe that is the product of soul; and time must precede motion, in the order of nature, because we say that motion is in time, which is conceived by Plotinus as something substantial. This substantial existence of time is doubtless influenced by Plato's tendency to speak of time as possessing an objective existence, but it is especially due to the nature of Plotinus' own system, which considers everything as existing in something else that is prior in nature and causality. With the interposition of soul between eternity and time the concept of life becomes very convenient to explain how time is an image of eternity. There are other terms that possess the flexibility that "life" does, but it is

[31] Cf. the treatise on numbers, vi. 6. Time is said to imitate eternity at i. 5. 7, v. 1. 4, and vi. 5. 11, but not in terms of number.

chosen apparently because time is connected with the motion of the universe, and it is more adaptable than the term "motion." For Plotinus' dialectic makes use of the five highest categories of the *Sophist*, and a place is found for them in intellect. If intellect, therefore, is to be eternal, eternity cannot be explained in terms of motion, since motion is only one of the five categories. "Life" thus becomes more suitable because it is more general than "motion."

Time is an image of eternity, therefore, as life on a lower level of perfection. Its striving to be as like eternity as possible is the reason for its constant progress, in order that it may be a whole in succession as eternity is a perfect whole without succession. This striving explains why time will never end, for its complete fulfillment is always beyond it. Time does not proceed according to number because ideal number is fixed at a higher level, and to think that soul produces in accordance with number conflicts with the infinity of time. Plotinus, as a matter of fact, does not stress the metaphor whereby time is called an image of eternity, for he is more concerned with showing how they differ.

This is an inherent characteristic of the Plotinian method. Everything that exists in the hierarchy of being must be like its cause, but the fact that there is something produced by a cause makes it necessary that the differences between the two be emphasized. Thus one of his favorite devices is the application of a pair of contraries to the higher and the lower objects of his discussion. This is in accord with the natural descent of things from a first principle through intermediaries, because the reason that such a descent is possible depends upon the capacity of the product to differentiate itself from the cause. Moreover, when the mind reverses the natural order and ascends from the lower to the higher it does so by passing from one contrary to the other, in this manner leaving ever behind the less perfect. So here Plotinus will explain the differences between time and eternity in terms of contraries, all of them applied to the concept of life, which suffers in its function of model and image and tends to become a background against which the differences between time and eternity are clearly perceived.

The fact that Plotinus places time in a hierarchy of being involving a descent that may be described by means of contraries results in another important difference between the time of Plotinus and of Plato. For Plotinus time is an intermediate between eternity (or the higher soul that contemplates eternity) and the motion of the universe that manifests time as the creative power of soul. Thus time is considered as a step in the descent of being from the more to the less perfect. In order for time and the universe to exist, soul must descend from the contemplation of eternity to the production of something inferior to itself. This offers Plotinus an opportunity in other contexts to speak of time as something that the soul of man must rise above in order to attain perfection. For Plato, however, time does not have this downward tendency. Although he would surely agree to some extent with Plotinus about man's obligation to rise above a temporal universe, his discussion of time proceeds in such a way that time is considered as a means whereby world and man become more perfect. Time is placed by Plato's dialectic along with number as an intermediary between the unity of eternity and the sheer multiplicity of becoming. The function of time is to assimilate the realm of becoming to that of being. No distinction is made between time and the motion of the universe because this motion proceeding according to number is the mean between the unity of eternal being and the indiscriminate motion of becoming. When we look at the numbers of the heavenly motions, therefore, we are to see in them the likeness of this universe to an eternal model. Insofar as time has a moral significance for Plato, it is a good one, for we are able to lead a better life by observing these numbers and adjusting the motions within our soul to the perfect motions of the heavenly bodies.

When we say that in Plato no distinction is made between time and the motion of the heavenly bodies, it must not be thought that this is an invariable view of time for Plato. Rather in the context in which time is explained Plato sets up a framework of terms and images among which time is given a certain place, and the significance that time is intended to have in this context is determined by its relation to other terms. These terms are different for Plato and for Plotinus because the former does not have hypostases or other fixed points of reference possessing the stability to be found in Plotinus. In another context, therefore, Plato might well have found it desirable to distinguish time very carefully from the motion of the universe, but his purpose here is to show that time has the function of assimilating motion, which does not in itself possess regularity or order, to eternity, and in this way indicate that time is a bridge, as it were, linking the realms of being and becoming, with the emphasis on the upward tendency of the universe resulting from its becoming temporal.

Plotinus also explains time with reference to other terms that he arranges in a context according to his own dialectic. Thus time is to be understood in its relation to soul and to the motion of the universe as well as to eternity. Again we must not expect a very strict definition of time, because the "motion" and "soul" are themselves incapable of strict definition and may be used in a rather wide range. When we consider soul, however, and the other hypostases, intellect and the One, we find that their range of application is more limited than that of other terms, especially as we go higher in the dialectic, because these are points of reference for all other terms, and, moreover, they are fixed invariably with reference to one another. Thus, while time cannot be given a strict definition, its position in the Plotinian hierarchy can be approximately determined by means of the hypostases. It is for this reason that we have said that time hovers between soul and the motion of the universe. Everything that Plotinus has said and will say about time, for example, that through soul it is an image of eternity and a life that progresses by a kind of extension, serves to indicate that in the hierarchy it is to be thought of as subsequent to soul and prior to the motion of the universe. Insofar as it is said to be the life in which the motion of the universe exists it is considered from the standpoint of soul, since soul is the cause of the universe. But when we think of time as having succession and ever new actualization, we are thinking of it from the standpoint of the motion that exists in it, for soul in itself is without succession. In this way Plotinus can give us a description that resembles a definition but can only approximate the strictness and fixity of an Aristotelian definition.

### PLOTINUS AND ARISTOTLE

Now that Plotinus has told us what he means by time we can see more clearly why he was not satisfied with Aristotle's explanation. Aristotle arrived at his definition of time as the number or measure of motion by means of an analysis that proceeded from nature and motion to time within a very narrow framework. Since motion is characteristic of nature, which is the subject matter of the *Physics*, motion and other things which seem to be related to motion are discussed insofar as they fall within the province of the physical philosopher and can be examined by the method proper to this science. This method is empirical and demands that we proceed from the rather confused phenomena that are presented to our senses and bring order into our knowledge by reducing the phenomena to the principles and causes that underlie them. We do not begin the study of nature by showing how it is derived from a higher realm of being, because we go in the other direction; nor do we approach time by deriving it from eternity. We simply examine motion and time in the same isolation in which they are presented by nature to our elementary observation. We discover that time is something by which we number or measure the succession that exists in motion, and this is the reason for our definition.

In the same manner we can examine various attributes of time. As our analysis proceeds we can trace all motion back to circular motion, which, being the only motion that can be eternally uniform, is now recognized to be the motion of which time is primarily the measure. Later still we can supplement our analysis by actual observation of the heavens and say that the motion of the outer heaven fulfills the requirements laid down in our analysis and is therefore the explanation of all other motion and of the uniformity of time. But none of these later discussions can affect the validity of the definition arrived at earlier by the proper method; they simply offer a clear explanation in the light of causes and principles why the definition is as we discovered it to be. For this reason the statement of Bréhier that the fundamental difference between Aristotle and Plotinus is that the latter believes in the world soul can hardly be right.[32] Whether the ultimate reason for the existence of time is the revolution of the outer heaven or a world soul, Aristotle's definition remains the same. That is to say, even if Aristotle had agreed with Plotinus that a world soul produced the universe, time for him would still be the number of motion.

Plotinus, not unlike Bréhier, evaluates Aristotle's view out of relation to the method that produced it. Plotinus approaches the problem of time as a firm believer in the hierarchy of hypostases and in the production of the universe through the causality exercised by them. His method is to proceed rather empirically up to a certain point, and, as we saw, he criticized certain views of time in a fashion very similar to that of Aristotle. When he comes to Aristotle, however, he finds that the other's definition is inadequate because, in effect, it tells us what time does, not what time is. For Aristotle this is entirely adequate, for according to the procedure he follows the definition of time can only tell us the relation of time to motion, and this involves the functioning of time as a number or measure. Plotinus, however, must demand that we say what time is in itself, which means for him what position time holds in the hierarchy of being. Proceeding by an upward path, we can discover that motion manifests time and time leads us to eternity by reminiscence. Descending now in the same way in which time descended we can attach time to eternity through the intermediation of soul, and we now know what time is, because we have determined its relation to its causes, and until we do this we do not know what time is in its essence.

Plotinus' criticism of Aristotle, as we noted, is based on his own presupposition of the proper method one should use in arriving at a knowledge of time. As he will say later,

[32] *Op. cit.*, p. 126.

Aristotle tells us only of an accidental characteristic of time, that it is a measure of motion. For its essence is not to be determined by the way in which we use it. We may also apply numbers to time, but this does not affect its essential nature. Nor does he approve, as we have seen, of relating the prior and posterior in time to the prior and posterior in motion and in space, as Aristotle's physical analysis does, since there can be no motion in space for Plotinus unless soul's activity is responsible for it. Thus Plotinus is looking for a metaphysically existing time, and his criticism of Aristotle implies that he too is or should be looking for the same kind of being.

### TIME AND THE DIVINE HYPOSTASES

The derivation of time from eternity cannot be understood without reference, as Plotinus has explained, to the descent of soul from the intellectual realm to the production of the universe. Just as eternity is the life of intellect, so time is the life of soul considered as having separated itself from intellect and entered an existence that involves succession and change. We can call intellect earlier than time and soul if we remember that intellect is prior in dignity and soul is dependent upon it as the third divine hypostasis. "Earlier" in the temporal sense is generated by time, and in time there is a striving, for the future, that is part of the nature of time. When soul reposes in contemplation of intellect, then time reposes also, but of course when so reposing it is not time. Time can be said to repose in the sense that the whole temporal order is somehow implicit in the power of soul, but it is not until soul begins to exercise its power that time really begins to exist (though this beginning must not be understood to mean that there was a first moment of time).

But Plotinus must explain why soul did not always remain in contemplation of intellect, which contains all being with utmost perfection and eternal life. This explanation will also tell us why time exists instead of the immutability of the intellectual life. We must think of a power of soul which, considered in somewhat anthropomorphic terms, was not satisfied with mere contemplation of being which was perfect, infinite, and eternally self-contained. This power was anxious to produce a universe which, through the activity of soul, would contain multiplicity and succession instead of eternal unity, but which, nevertheless, would imitate the eternal realm as far as this is possible to a world of change. Soul in the mere contemplation of intellect is like the seed which is at rest, and contains implicitly the order of the complete plant. From the seed a creative principle unwinds itself and from the self-contained unity of the seed there emerges the plant with its many parts. Such apparent progress to the plurality of the manifold creation that results from the activity of the creative principle is productive of weakness rather than of strength; for the whole perfection of the plant was in the seed in a state of unity, but now that unity has been diffused and the seed no longer possesses it. In similar fashion a power of soul was not content with reposing in the upper world of intellect. It was eager to translate into a world of multiplicity the perfect unity of intelligible being which was within its grasp, and the product of its activity was the sensible world which it produces in imitation of the intelligible world that it contemplates. However, as Plotinus often insists, not all soul has descended to production, but a part of it, a higher soul, must remain in contemplation of intellect; otherwise, soul would be cut off from the source of its power, and its productive activity would cease.

The life of thought which the soul has when it descends into the realm of multiplicity and produces its effects in imitation of the intelligible world (which a part of it never ceases to contemplate) effects the becoming of time. Time, which was previously implicit in the power of soul before that power became actually engaged in production, now moves along with this new, extended life of soul as a line is generated from a point, and thus time exists in imitation of eternity. In order for soul to produce the many effects of which it is capable it must descend from a state in which it only contemplates eternity and must now make itself in a sense temporal. This is not putting its own life in time, for this new mode of life *is* time. But all its effects in the sensible universe must be in time, for soul produces everything through its own life and in that life. Thus the universe and all its development must be in time, because there can be no motion of any kind in the universe that does not have soul as its principle. This life of soul is one of thought, in which it produces its effects by translating into multiplicity the world of being that it contemplates. It is this activity of thought that produces succession in the universe by constantly receiving new actualization (from the standpoint of the universe, as has been said). Thus time progresses with the life of soul, for it is the life of soul as this life passes onward unceasingly.

Plotinus has systematized various statements of Plato to arrive at his three divine hypostases. In the light of the hypostases eternity is explained at length as the life of intellect reposing in the One and directed towards it; this is adapted from Plato's statement that eternity reposes in unity while time proceeds according to number.[33] So Plotinus systematizes the Platonic discussion of time in terms of his three

[33] *Timaeus* 37d.

hypostases. If eternity is the life of the intelligible world, which Plotinus says it is on the basis of certain statements of Plato, then time, which is called by Plato the image of eternity, must be the life of soul, which is not said explicitly by Plato at all. Plotinus, like Plato, explains time by showing where it exists in the hierarchy of being, but since his hierarchy is more fixed and rigid than Plato's, so time can more readily be given a fixed position.

### TIME AS THE IMAGE OF ETERNITY

Plotinus now proceeds to show more clearly how time is the image of eternity (11. 45). If eternity is life that exists in repose, identity, and self-contained infinity, and time must be considered as its image, just as this sensible universe imitates the intelligible, then instead of the intellectual life we must think of time as another life belonging to this creative power of soul, a life that is so called by a kind of equivocation in relation to the intellectual life. Instead of the motion proper to intellect there is the motion of a part of soul; instead of self-identity and permanence, change and activity that is ever different; instead of the indivisible and one, an image that is one only in continuity; instead of self-contained infinity and completeness, that which proceeds to infinity by unending succession; instead of that which is a whole all at once, that which is a whole by coming into existence part by part and by always so coming into existence. In this way will time imitate the infinite and perfect completeness of intellect, so long as it will strive for greater and greater addition to its being; for its being imitates in this way the being of intellect. We must not think, then, that time is outside of soul any more than in the realm of intellect eternity is outside of being. It is not a mere accompaniment or consequent upon soul, but, being analogous to eternity, it is manifested in soul, dwells within it, and is united to it.

Plotinus thus explains time more fully by showing its relation to eternity, from which it is derived in the hierarchy of being. Just as this sensible universe imitates the intelligible world, so time, which is the life of soul in the universe, imitates eternity, the life of intellect. Time is an image, first of all, because it is a kind of life. It is life only in a somewhat equivocal sense of the word, because true life belongs to intellect, but it can be called life because in the productive activity which distinguishes this phase of soul time with its succession and change has a position analogous to that of eternity in intellect. Only by substituting a temporal existence for the eternal is this power of soul able to translate perfect being into a world of division and multiplicity. Thus time is the life of soul as eternity is the life of intellect. Intellect has in it a kind of motion, which is the life of thought, but this motion is so perfect that its activity involves no change or succession, because its object is present all at once; so a part of soul has in it a motion which is analogous but different, because its activity is not identical always with itself. This life of soul is not one indivisibly, but imitates the indivisible unity of intellectual life by having oneness in continuity. This life is also infinite and a whole, but only by continuously achieving its being, for it is thus that it imitates the self-contained unity of true being. If time is an image of this kind, then clearly it cannot be in any way extraneous or accidental to soul, but exists along with it as its very life, just as eternity exists in intellect. The systematic adaptation of Plato continues in this passage. Time considered as the motion of a part of soul, for example, is said to imitate the motion of intellect, which is eternal. This motion of intellect and true being, which Plotinus has already discussed as one of the five aspects of eternity, seems to be taken from the *Sophist*, where motion is given as one of the five highest genera. Plato says nothing of this motion, however, when describing how time is an image of eternity.

### TIME AND THE LIFE OF SOUL

Time, continues Plotinus, considered as the extension of the life of soul, a prolongation consisting in changes that take place quietly and with regularity and uniformity, has a continuous flow of activity (12. 1). Let us suppose that this power could turn back and cease from its present life, the life which is really unceasing and will never fail because it is the activity of a soul that is always, and an activity that is not self-centered, but producing and generating. If we could suppose that this activity would cease and that this part of soul would return to the intellectual realm and eternity, and remain there in tranquillity, how could there be anything in existence after eternity? How could there be change if all things were to remain in unity? Why should there be an "earlier," or rather, why a "later"? There would be nothing to which soul could direct its attention, not even eternal being; for soul would have to withdraw from this being in order to direct its attention toward it, instead of being unified with it through contemplation.

Having shown that if time should cease (which can never happen) soul would no longer exercise the activities of production proper to it and there would be nothing but the immutable tranquillity of eternal being, Plotinus says that neither would there be the celestial sphere to receive the attention of soul, because this did not exist before time. For it exists and has its motion in time, and even if it should come to rest we should be able to measure the extent of this rest, as long as soul is acting outside of eternity. If, therefore, the withdrawal of soul and its unification in eternity would destroy time, it is clear that it was the descent of soul to the motion of this lower realm that generated time. Plato says that time came into existence along with the universe. The reason for this is that soul generated time and the universe together. For in this activity of soul the universe was generated as well as time, and this activity is time, while the universe is in time.

Plotinus thus indicates that the celestial sphere exists and moves in time because it is produced by an activity of soul descending from the simple perfection of eternity, and we must look upon time as producing the sphere rather than the reverse. For even if the motion of the sphere should cease, we could measure the extent of its rest, provided soul were still active. Plotinus would have to admit, for reasons that we shall see, that soul would be able to measure this rest of the celestial sphere only by means of some other motion generated by soul's activity capable of providing a unit of measure, because in its own life there is perfect continuity, which of itself cannot measure anything. He wants to show here merely that time is dependent for its existence not upon the motion of the celestial sphere, but upon the activity of soul. The interpretation of Plato's statement that time began with the universe is in Plotinian terms, according to which time and the universe are both generated by soul's activity, for time is this activity and the universe is in it, and this activity of soul implies the universe as a necessary product. So time and the universe must exist together, the former as that in which the universe exists, the latter as the product that necessarily results from the activity of soul called time. For Plato the universe is not said to be generated by soul's activity, and time is referred to the motions of the heavenly bodies rather than to any activity of soul.

## THE MEASUREMENT OF TIME

Plotinus proceeds to interpret other statements of Plato in the same systematic way (12.25). The statement that the motions of the stars are times [34] Plotinus conveniently interprets with the aid of other quotations from Plato. We should remember, he says, that the stars came into existence in order to manifest and distinguish time,[35] and in order that there might be a clear measure.[36] Because it was impossible for soul to distinguish time in itself and for men unaided to number the parts of time, since it cannot be seen or grasped, and especially since men did not know how to number, Plato tells us that God made day and night, so that it was now possible to comprehend the number two through their difference, from which comes our conception of number.[37]

Since time is an activity of soul for Plotinus, he can use the heavenly bodies only to manifest time and to distinguish parts of time that in itself it does not have. In no way will he permit us to say that time is generated by the motions of the heavenly bodies, for they exist and move *in* time. The activity of soul progresses uniformly and quietly, Plotinus has previously said, and soul can therefore make no distinction or differentiation in time itself, although it can in things produced in time. Moreover, men, if left to rely on themselves, cannot measure time because it is invisible and intangible. They must therefore use the heavenly motions to make time manifest to themselves and to divide it into equal

---

[34] Adapted from *ibid*. 39d.

[35] Plato says that they came into existence to distinguish and guard the numbers of time, *ibid*. 38c.

[36] Plato says this of the sun, *ibid*. 39b.

[37] Adapted from *ibid*. 39b, 47a.

parts.[38] In addition, men could not number before they received their concept of number from observing the heavens.[39] For these reasons the motions of the heavenly bodies are important for man's perception of time, but they are not themselves time. It is interesting to note that Plotinus omits Plato's statement that the stars guard the numbers of time, especially when we find no mention of time proceeding according to number, which Plato stresses.

Since Plotinus has made time the continuous and undifferentiated life of soul, it cannot have numbers in it, and the concept of number that we receive from observation of the heavens helps us only to measure the activity of soul but has no intrinsic connection with time itself. Plotinus in thus departing from Plato has omitted one very important way in which time for Plato is an image of eternity, that is, the regular procession of a numerical series imitating the changeless unity of eternity. Plotinus would surely find difficulty with such a series in time, just as he asked of the Aristotelian view how time, being infinite, could have a number unless we take only a part of it. At any rate, he would doubtless think that the undivided flow of soul's activity is a better imitation of eternal unity than a numerical series would be.[40]

Plotinus now proceeds to tell more explicitly how we measure time (12. 33). By taking the extension of motion from one sunrise to the next we can arrive at the extension of time which has elapsed, because the motion on which we are relying is uniform, and thus we avail ourselves of a measure. But we see that we have here a measure *of* time,

---

[38] In his next chapter Plotinus shows more clearly how time is manifested by celestial motion.

[39] Plotinus interprets this more fully in vi. 6. 4.

[40] Even the motion of the heaven in a sense is one; it is we who divide its single day into many days, iv. 4. 7.

for time itself is not a measure. For how could time, being an unbroken continuity, measure anything by proclaiming that the thing measured was as great as a part of itself? Rather there is a measuring in terms of time (such as three days), and in this sense we can use time for measuring, but it is not in itself a measure. We can say that the motion of the universe is measured in terms of time. But even so time will not be a measure of motion in its own essence; rather, being previously something else in its essence, it will incidentally inform us of the quantity of the motion. By taking a single motion (such as that of the universe) in a definite extension of time, and numbering this motion again and again, we come to know how much time has passed. Thus we see that motion, in particular the circular motion of the heaven, in some fashion provides a measure for time. This it does by manifesting in a definite quantity of itself a definite extension of time, and this can be grasped and perceived in no other way. Time, therefore, will be measured and in that way manifested to us by the celestial motion, but not generated by it.

Time is a measure of motion (12. 52) insofar as it has itself been measured by a definite motion, and as measured by this motion it must be considered different from it. Just as we saw that time insofar as it measures motion is different from it, so is time different insofar as it is measured, and the fact that it is measured by motion is also incidental. To say that time is essentially something measured by motion would be as if someone should define magnitude as that which is measured by a cubit-rule, without telling what it is essentially, or as if someone, finding that he could not give a definition of motion, should call it that which is measured by space, reckoning the extent of the motion from the space it has traversed.

## THE MANIFESTATION OF TIME BY MOTION

Having shown thus the relationship of the heavenly motions to time, Plotinus proceeds to point out more clearly how time is manifested to us by these motions, especially the circular motion of the heaven (13. 1). This circular motion, as we have seen, manifests time to us because it is in time, while time, in the realm of things that come after intellect, is first, being the life of the productive soul, and in this realm there is nothing prior to it in which it exists. It is in time that other things move and remain at rest with regularity and order. (Plotinus would admit, however, that there are some irregular motions, but these are irrelevant to his present purpose. It is difficult to see how a state of rest as such can be other than regular, but we might call it irregular if it is continually interrupted by motion.) From something that exhibits order, whether it be moving or at rest, time appears and manifests itself to our thought, but time itself is not generated in this way. This manifestation takes place more readily if the object is moving, for motion is more capable of leading us to a recognition and perception of time than rest, and the extent to which a thing has moved is more obvious than the extent to which a thing has been at rest.

For Plotinus time, as we see, is the hidden life of soul that provides the sensible universe with motion. We are able to perceive this life through its manifestation in nature; and from natural motions, especially that of the celestial sphere, we can be made aware of the flow of time. Time shines out with especial clarity from a thing that possesses an orderly motion, because such a motion follows most closely the pattern provided by time itself. Thus the most important medium in nature for the perception of time is the uniform motion of the celestial sphere, which is moved by the life of the world soul within. This world soul, which desires to attain the ultimate Good that intellect already contemplates, causes the body into which it infuses life to move in a circle, and this motion about a fixed point represents the desire of soul to possess the Good, which is the center and source of all being. For this reason the celestial motion reveals so well the flow of time, which is the life of soul within.[41] Other motions may also manifest time, but none so well as this motion. These other motions must be uniform as far as that is possible, for the more uniformity a motion possesses the more clearly does the uniform flow of time shine forth. Even an object at rest, we are now told, may manifest time, because a thing rests in time and this persistence in time somehow gives us a perception of time itself. Plotinus does not say, as Aristotle would, that time pertains to rest only by virtue of a contemporary motion. He seems to think that an object which rests in time may manifest the time in which it rests to the perceiver; it does not do this, however, so clearly as motion, because time itself, considered as life, is a kind of motion.

Plotinus does not give us many details of the psychological process by which we perceive time as it is thus manifested to us. He does indicate elsewhere that memory is employed whenever we perceive the flow of time.[42] This would mean that successive aspects of motion retained in memory manifest the passage of time to us (and presumably also successive aspects of rest, but Plotinus does not say what these aspects of rest would be). This mention of memory, which foreshadows St. Augustine, makes explicit

[41] Cf. iv. 4. 16, ii. 2, vi. 5. 11.

[42] iv. 4. 8. A view of time that has psychological implications is also set forth in i. 5.

what is implied by Aristotle in making time a number, for this too would be impossible if there were no memory. For Plotinus, however, this observation of various aspects of motion only manifests time, which exists independently of the observation.

It is this close connection between time and motion, continues Plotinus, and the fact that we can reckon the extent of motion in terms of time that led some philosophers to say that time is the measure of motion (13. 9). They should have said rather that it is measured by motion, and then added what this thing is essentially that is so measured; instead of this they offer only an accidental characteristic of time and this in opposite fashion. But perhaps they really do not mean to be understood in this opposite fashion; it may be that it is their intention to use the term "measure" with all clarity in the sense of something that is measured and we do not grasp their meaning.[43] The reason that we are unable to understand their meaning more precisely is that in their writings they do not make clear what time is in itself, whether measuring or measured, since they were writing for followers who knew their doctrine.

Plato, however, continues Plotinus, does not say that time is essentially something that measures or is measured, but that it is merely manifested to us by the correspondence of the smallest part of the celestial revolution to the smallest portion of time, so that we can learn therefrom something of the character of time and of its quantity. When he wants to indicate the essence of time he says that it came into existence along with the heaven, having eternity as its

---

[43] Plotinus seems to have in mind especially the passage of Aristotle, *Physics* 220b14–32, where time and motion are said to measure each other. This admission of Aristotle is inclined to make Plotinus more lenient toward him, unless we are to consider Plotinus as indulging in irony.

model and being a moving image of it; for time does not stand still as long as the life of soul, with which time progresses, does not, and it is this one life that fashions both the universe and time. If this life should return to unity, then time, existing in this life, would have ceased along with it, and the heaven also, having this life no longer.

This reference of Plotinus to Plato is interesting in that it offers explicitly the two ways in which we know time, the contrast between them having been implied in the previous discussion. Since time as the life of soul is invisible to us, it must be manifested by the motions produced by it, and in particular by the circular motion of the heaven. We can think of the flow of time as being reflected very clearly in the uniform motion of the heaven because this motion is the primary manifestation of the life of the world soul. The chief danger, Plotinus thinks, is that because of the close relation of this motion to the world soul we might think that this motion is time or produces time. Rather we should be led by the uniformity of this motion to the perception of time as the power that motivates the heaven. This motion, therefore, tells us something of the general character of time, namely, that it is a hidden power that is manifesting itself to us in this motion; this motion can likewise enable us to measure time, which we should be unable to do otherwise even if we could perceive time without this manifestation of it. But this perception does not tell us what time is in its very essence. To know this we must know what position time holds in the hierarchy of being, and thus we must go back to eternity, from which time is derived. From our perception of time we are led by reminiscence to eternity, which Plotinus discussed in the opening chapters of this treatise; such a discussion presupposed that he had already ascended to the world of intellect by means of reminiscence.

Then he was able to derive time from eternity in his discussion just as in the natural order of things time descends from eternity. Only in this way can we arrive at a knowledge of time's essence, as Plotinus has done at some length, by deriving time from eternity as a moving image, through the medium of soul. The statements of Plato are adapted to fit this distinction of Plotinus, but this adaptation is by no means a violent distortion.

### THE REALITY OF TIME

If someone, continues Plotinus, considering the prior and posterior of the life and motion of the universe, should call this time, since it does have some reality, and then say that the truer motion of soul with its prior and posterior has no reality, he would be most foolish (13. 30). For this would be granting to a motion which is not that of soul the exclusive possession of prior and posterior and of time, while not granting this to the motion in imitation of which this other motion exists, and from which the prior and posterior first came to be. This higher motion acts through its own power and generates, as it were, its own acts and their succession. Why, then, in referring the motion of the universe to this higher motion by which it is enveloped do we say that it is in time, and yet do not say this of the motion of soul which has within soul an everlasting procession? The reason is that before soul there is eternity, whose unity does not permit it to be coextensive with the progress of soul. Soul, therefore, was the first to descend to time by generating time and possessing it along with its own activity. Why, then, is time everywhere? Because soul is absent from no part of the universe, just as the soul within us is absent from no part of us.

It is interesting to note how the position of time in the

hierarchy of being is determined by Plotinus. The motion
of the universe, first of all, is called an imitation of the
higher motion of soul, just as this motion of soul is a moving
image of eternity, the life of intellect which itself possesses
the perfect motion of pure thought. Since motion has such
a wide range of application, it is clear that time could not
be given a fixed position if it depended only on motion.
Moreover, just as the universe exists in the life of soul, so
soul may in a sense be said to exist in intellect, and intellect
in the ultimate unity which is beyond all being.[44] In fact,
all beings may be said to exist somehow in this ultimate
hypostasis, since otherwise they would be cut off from the
source of all being. Thus "having existence in" something
which is a source of being or activity cannot provide a de-
terminate position for time any more than the concept of
motion can. Plotinus can determine the position of time,
and therefore its essential nature, only by means of his
hypostases. It is the life of soul considered as producing the
universe, and is not any other motion than this life; the
universe exists in time, but soul does not because before
soul there is not this life of soul. Thus time is fixed and
stabilized because the hypostases are points of reference
that are fixed and stable for Plotinus, not completely so,
since being really descends from the One without a break
in its continuity, but at least in relation to one another.

If anyone should say, continues Plotinus, that time consists in something that has no subsistence or existence, then
he will clearly belie the existence of God himself whenever
he says that God was or will be (13. 49). For God was and
will be only insofar as that thing is in which this person says
God was or will be.

This argument seems to be directed against a view of

[44] Cf. v. 5. 9.

time such as that of Aristotle, a view that makes time to be a kind of abstraction and not a really existing thing. This attenuated time is repugnant to Plotinus and would certainly be repugnant, he says, to the man who proclaims that God was and will be, and therefore exists in time, if he should think of the consequences of making time a mere abstraction. This same difficulty applies also to other things which are said to be in time. As a matter of fact, Plotinus would not himself think of God as existing in time, to whichever of the hypostases the term be applied. For this reason he concludes the discussion by saying that those who say that God was and will be should be answered by another kind of argument. But his immediate purpose is merely to show the consequences of making time an abstraction for those things that exist in time, and to show, by implication, the disagreement between this view and that of men in general, who frequently employ temporal expressions even of God.[45]

### THE UNITY OF TIME

There is one further point to be considered, continues Plotinus (13. 53). Whenever we observe how far a man who is moving has progressed, then we also observe the quantity of his motion, and from the quantity of his motion, such as walking, we can perceive the quantity of the vital impulse existing in the man as the cause of the motion, a quantity that corresponds with that of his bodily motion. In similar fashion the fact that his body moves for a certain length of time we can refer to the time of the corresponding motion (for this motion is the cause of the man's being

---

[45] If we are to attribute the view here criticized by Plotinus to the Gnostics, then the criticism is more pointed, but the interpretation remains essentially the same.

in motion), and then we can refer this motion's being in a certain time to the motion of his soul, which has a corresponding extension.

To what, then, shall we refer the motion of the soul? Whatever it is, it will be without extension, for among things that have extension the motion of soul is that which is first and in which other things have their motion, and in this realm there is nothing in which it exists.[46] What we have said about the motion of the man's soul applies in the same manner to the soul of the universe. If we say, therefore, that time is the life of soul, manifested especially by the motion of the heaven, are we to think that time is also within men because of their souls? We must answer that time is in everything that has the nature of soul, being the same in kind in all souls, for in a sense all souls are one. For this reason time will not be dispersed, just as eternity is not dispersed in belonging to beings that are the same in kind, though not in the same way as time belongs to soul.[47]

This last section of the text offers an important addition to the account of time given by Plotinus. We were previously told that time was generated by soul, but especial emphasis was placed on the soul of the universe in view of the fact that the celestial revolution was set forth as the best manifestation of the productive activity of soul. At this point we come to the explicit consideration of time in individual souls. We find that the actions of a man have a temporal duration that may be traced back ultimately to the motion of his soul, for before this soul there is eternity,

---

[46] So previously we were told that time, which is the life of soul, is in a certain way first, and other things move in it, 13. 1–4.

[47] The reasons given by Fritz Heinemann, *Plotin* (Leipzig: F. Meiner. 1921), pp. 96–98, to show that this last section is not authentic and not capable of consistent explanation seem to be either irrelevant or based on a wrong interpretation of the text.

which is without any extension whatsoever and is consequently outside the range of our present discussion. Thus the motion of the individual soul is not in time; rather it generates time for this individual, and each individual has his own duration, just as the soul of the universe has the time which is generated by itself. But this does not mean that there are many different times, for there is but one nature of soul, and, though each soul will have its own duration, still there will be a common duration for all souls. This is another way of saying what Plotinus has already mentioned, namely, that there is time everywhere in the universe because soul is present everywhere, just as, by analogy, our soul is present in every part of us.

Plotinus in this way reconciles the individuality of the particular soul with the unity of nature possessed by all that is soul.[48] There is a kind of sympathy existing between particular souls and the soul of the universe because they are derived from the same nature of soul.[49] Plotinus says in another place that time may be said to have been generated by the soul of the universe;[50] his reason doubtless is that the heavenly motion is, as he has often stated, the best manifestation of the life of soul. But even our souls are eternal, he continues, just as the soul of the universe is, and time is something that is posterior in nature to all soul. Thus in the case of the individual soul its affections and productions may be said to be in time, but the soul itself is not. It is clear, therefore, that Plotinus is careful to preserve the analogy between our souls and the soul of the universe. There is a numerically different time, we may say, for each soul, but time is the same in kind everywhere because the

[48] This point is of concern to him elsewhere; cf. iv. 3. 1–8.
[49] Cf. iv. 3. 8.
[50] iv. 4. 15.

nature of soul is the same (though our souls are by no means parts of the world soul), just as eternity, belonging in its own way to every being in the world of intellect, remains one nevertheless.

This same analogy shows us that time should not be thought of as subjective for Plotinus in the sense that its existence depends on our knowing it. It is not in this way that our souls are said to have time, for we possess a duration in the life of our souls even when we are unaware of it. Rather time has a metaphysical subsistence in our souls just as it has in the soul of the universe, and, therefore, its existence is prior to the knowledge of the individual man. Moreover, we should be slow to read into Plotinus "not a sensible but an intimate, *a priori* experience of that life which is time" [51] in the case of individual souls, since Plotinus stresses the point that time is manifested to us by motion, especially the regular motion of the heaven.

[51] Clark, *op. cit.*, p. 352.

# 4

# AUGUSTINE

## *Time, a Distention of Man's Soul*

THE PROBLEM of time has a number of different aspects in St. Augustine, but it is in the eleventh book of the *Confessions*, beginning with the fourteenth chapter, that he asks himself explicitly what time is and tries to answer the question. After recounting in ten books the history of his former life, especially his inner life and spiritual struggles, he devotes three books to an exposition of the opening words of Genesis. This exposition, in which he "confesses" his present state of mind with regard to the words of Scripture,[1] offers St. Augustine an opportunity for praising the works of God and beseeching further enlightenment concerning God's mysteries; but above all he hopes to arouse in himself and in others a greater love of God.[2]

### GOD AND CREATION

The words of Scripture relating to creation are corroborated by the changeable nature of heaven and earth, which are said to have been created in the beginning by God; for

---

[1] *Confessions* xi. 2, et olim inardesco meditari in lege tua et in ea tibi confiteri scientiam et inperitiam meam.
[2] *Ibid.* 1.

that which changes cannot be eternal.[3]  St. Augustine now
considers those who ask what God was doing before He
made heaven and earth.[4]  Men who ask such a question
clearly do not have any knowledge whatsoever of things
eternal.  Since God is the creator of time as well as of
heaven and earth, there could have been no time before
God's act of creation.  Since there was no time before
heaven and earth existed, it is useless to ask what God was
doing then; for there was no "then" when there was no
time.[5]  It is true that God precedes all time; He does not,
however, precede time temporally, but through the eminence of eternal existence, which is altogether present and
involves no future or past.[6]

When there was no time, therefore, St. Augustine insists,
God had not made anything, because He is the author of
time itself.  No expanse of time is co-eternal with God, because He persists in eternity, while time by its very nature
cannot persist in the present.  These considerations of God's
eternity and of the temporal nature of created things lead
St. Augustine to ask what this thing called time is, and his
investigation occupies a large part of the eleventh book.
He notes the difficulty that one encounters when one attempts to grasp the nature of time so as to offer a definition
of it (chap. 14).  There is nothing that we seem to know
better than time when we speak of it ourselves or hear
others speak of it.  If no one asks him what time is, says
St. Augustine, he knows what it is; but if he tries to explain
it to someone, he does not know what it is.

---

[3] *Ibid.* 4, clamant, quod facta sint; mutantur enim atque variantur.
[4] *Ibid.* 10–13, 30.
[5] *Ibid.* 13. Cf. *The City of God* xi. 4–6.
[6] *Confessions* xi. 11, non autem praeterire quicquam in aeterno, sed
totum esse praesens. Cf. *ibid.* 13.

### HOW PAST, PRESENT, AND FUTURE TIME EXIST

St. Augustine undertakes to discuss the problem of time in a manner similar to that of Aristotle, by considering various difficulties that are offered by a preliminary examination of time. We can affirm first of all that if nothing passed away, there would be no past time; if nothing came to be, there would be no future time; and if nothing existed at present, there would be no present time. This recognition that time is connected somehow with a flux of things is helpful as a first step in discovering what time is, but it also raises some difficulties. We may well wonder about the mode of existence possessed by the past and the future, since the past is no longer and the future is not yet. Even the present time is not altogether clear, because if it were always present and did not go into the past, this would not be time but eternity. St. Augustine will say later, as Aristotle does, that in a sense the present time always is, but he is saying here that the present, if it is to be time and not eternity, must have in it some kind of flux, since that which is present passes away and, existing no longer, is in the past. Therefore we may say that the present is time only if it goes into the past, and the reason for its existing as time is that it will not exist. Thus we find that while past and future time do not exist at all the present may truly be called time only because it tends to become nonexistent.

And yet, continues St. Augustine (chap. 15), in speaking of past and future time we refer either to a long time, such as a hundred years ago or a hundred years hence, or a short time, such as ten days ago or ten days hence. But since the past is no longer and the future is not yet, we may well wonder how that which does not exist can be either long or short. We should not say, therefore, that any past or future time is long, but that it was long, or will be long. But this raises a further difficulty. Taking past time into consideration, we find that it could not have been long when it was already past, because then it was no longer, and not existing it could not have been long. It could have been long only while it existed, that is, before it became past. Instead of saying, therefore, that a past time was long, as has been already suggested, we should say that it was long while it was still present, because as soon as it became past it ceased to exist and thereupon ceased to be long.

What St. Augustine has said about past time also applies to the future, which he discusses in a similar way somewhat later. It is clear, he thinks, that no time can be long unless it actually exists, unless, therefore, it is present. We must now consider whether present time can be long, hoping that any discovery we make about the length of time will lead us to a knowledge of time itself. St. Augustine here apostrophizes the human soul, calling upon it to answer his question whether present time can be long, for it is the soul that has the power to perceive and measure lapses of time. This apostrophe is in harmony with the introspective tone of the *Confessions* as a whole, and it is especially important, as will appear later, in the author's solution of the problem of time. Aristotle's view of time as a measure implied but did not explain very fully the psychological aspect of time. St. Augustine leaves us in no doubt as to the importance of a psychological approach to time.

Considering now whether present time can be long, let us look first at a period of a hundred years that is present and see whether it is long. But first we must ask whether a hundred years can really be present. For if we are in the first year of the century under consideration, the first year is present, to be sure, but the other ninety-nine are future and so do not yet exist. If we are in the second year, then that year is present, but one is past and the others are future. Similarly if we select any of the years that intervene between the first and last years of the century, it will be present, but those before it will be past, those after it future. We discover, therefore, that the period of a hundred years cannot be present. Let us turn from the century to that year which is now present, and again we find that the entire year is not present, but only one month of the twelve that compose the year. Looking at this month we find that only one day is present, with the other days coming after it, or before it, or both. Thus present time, which we previously said could alone be long, has now contracted from a century to the space of a single day. But this day has twenty-four hours, of which only one is present, and even the present hour is composed of fleeting moments which are not all present at once. If there is anything in time that cannot be divided any further into particles however small, then that deserves to be called present. But this present flies so swiftly from the future into the past that it contains no lapse or extension, for if it had extension (here St. Augustine and Aristotle agree) it could be divided, though presumably present, into past and future.

But if the present has no extension, where is the time that we call long? Since we saw that it could not be past perhaps it is future, in which case we should not say that it is long but that it will be long. But it will not be long while it is still future, for it will not yet exist in order to be long. So it will have to be long only when it has come from the future and become present, so that by existing it may be long. But we have just seen that the present cannot be long. Thus future time, as well as past time, cannot as such be long, because only that which exists can be long. But present time has no extension and for that reason cannot be long.

This conclusion, if it can be called such, does not seem to accord, St. Augustine says (chap. 16), with our experience, for we perceive intervals of time and compare them in length with one another. We are even able to measure how much longer or shorter one period of time is than another, as when we say that one period is twice or three times as long as another, or is equal to it. But when through our perception of time we measure periods of time, we do this only while they are passing. For if they are already past, or if they are future, then as such they cannot be measured, because one cannot measure that which is not. Time therefore can be perceived and measured only while it is passing.

Thus St. Augustine makes the problem more precise by showing that time must be considered as having some kind of extension in the present, even though we have previously seen that the present time seems to have no extension whatsoever. He does this by means of introspection, which tells us that we perceive and even measure extended intervals of time. But introspection and analysis tell us that we could not measure these intervals unless they were present, for otherwise they would not exist in order to be measured. This statement that an extended interval of time may somehow be present seems to contradict our previous conclusion that the present is without extension, but it is from this apparent paradox that St. Augustine will attempt to clarify the nature of time. His psychological approach, moreover, will provide the proper method by which to accomplish this end.

Our view that only the present exists seems to contradict,

St. Augustine continues (chap. 17), the accepted view of pedagogues that there are three times or tenses, past, present, and future. To save the existence of past and future someone might conceivably suggest that they really exist, but that the present emerges from some hidden place when it comes from the future into the present, and passes into another hidden place when it leaves the present for the past. To support this view that the past and future exist just as the present does, but are usually concealed from our consciousness, one might ask where those people who predict future events have seen them if they do not yet exist. For what does not exist cannot be seen. Moreover, when people recount past events, their speech would in no wise be truthful unless they saw these past events with their "mind's eye." But if these events did not exist they could not be seen at all. Thus it might be concluded that future and past events do exist.

But, says St. Augustine now (chap. 18), if these past and future events really exist, we might ask where they exist. Wherever they are, at any rate, they do not exist there as past or future, but as present. For if they are future there, they do not yet exist; if they are past there, they do not exist any longer. Therefore, wherever they are and whatever they are, they are only present. But St. Augustine is not satisfied with this one argument alone against the view that the past and future exist. He attempts to offer some explanation of these things themselves that appear to be past and future, and yet are really present. When someone is recounting past events, it is not the events themselves, which are past, that are brought forth from memory, but rather words that are formed from images of the events, since these events have left traces of themselves in the mind in passing through the senses. Thus one's boyhood, which is no longer, is in past time, which is no longer. But when it is recalled to mind and recounted, an image of it is contemplated in the present, because this image is still in the memory, though the event itself is not. Thus St. Augustine shows not only that whatever exists is present, though it may appear to be past, but also that what exists is not the past event itself but only an image of it, and that the place where it exists is the memory of the soul.

He is obliged, however, to admit that he is not certain whether future events can be predicted in a similar way, that is, merely through images of the events that are somehow perceived before the events themselves exist. There is something similar to such prediction whenever we premeditate a future action of our own, in which case the premeditation is present, but the action itself is still future. If we speak of a mysterious presentiment of the future, therefore, we may not be able to say how this takes place. But we are able to say that nothing can be perceived except that which exists, that which is present, not future. St. Augustine now shows that when we predict the future in the ordinary course of life the future events themselves, which do not yet exist, are not perceived, but only causes of these events or signs of some sort that foreshadow them. These causes or signs are present, not future, and by inference from them the future events are predicted by being conceived in the mind. These conceptions are also present as contemplated by those who predict the future. When I look at the dawn, for example, I predict that the sun will rise, and to do so I must have in my mind an image of the rising sun which I form on the basis of my observation. Both the dawn and the image of the rising sun that is in my mind are present, and from them I predict the rising of the sun, which is in the future. Thus future events, since they do not exist, cannot be perceived, but they can be predicted from present events which exist and are perceived.

St. Augustine now confesses briefly (chap. 19) that he does not know how God informed the ancient prophets of events to come. He suggests that God might have done this by giving them knowledge that was really present although it referred to future events. For He could not have taught them that which was not. Whether we predict the future, therefore, by means of inference from antecedents that already exist or in a more mysterious way, such as the prophets may have had, St. Augustine insists that nothing is ever really perceived unless it exists in the present, and is, moreover, somehow in the soul. Thus with the future as well as the past we find that the event which is future does not really exist, but is anticipated by means of some image in the soul that is present — although in predicting the future there is sometimes an element of mystery — and we have no more right to say that the future exists than the past. So St. Augustine disposes of the theory that the past and future exist in some place of concealment. The emphasis that he places on the soul's power to recall the past and anticipate the future though it exists in an indivisible present must be kept in mind when he comes to a positive explanation of time.

We must really hold, St. Augustine continues (chap. 20), contrary though it may seem to all we have been taught, that future and past events do not exist, and we should not say that there are three times, past, present, and future. It would perhaps be proper to say that there are three times, the present with reference to past events, the present with reference to present events, and the present with reference to future events. He insists that these three are in the soul and are not elsewhere, being a present memory of past events, a present attention to present events, and a present anticipation of future events. From his consideration that the past and future exist only in the memory and anticipation of the soul he has been led to say that even present time exists in the soul's attention, a psychological view of time that he will develop later. If we are permitted to offer this explanation of the three aspects of time, then he is willing to admit that in this sense there are three times, past, present, and future. Since our speech in general is not altogether precise, we may make this concession to popular custom, as long as we understand that the past and future do not as such really exist.

### THE MEASUREMENT OF TIME

St. Augustine now returns (chap. 21) to the subject of the measurement of time, which we can now discuss more fruitfully perhaps since we have seen in what sense past, present, and future time exist. We measure intervals of time while they are passing, as we saw before, so that we are able to say that one interval is twice as long as another, or is equal to another, or offer some other pronouncement about the parts of time. If someone should ask how we know that we measure intervals of time while they are passing, St. Augustine answers that from experience we know that we actually measure intervals of time, and reason tells us that we cannot measure what does not exist, as past and future do not. But if the interval of time that is measured is passing in the present, and is present, there is the difficulty that we have mentioned previously: how are we going to measure present time, which is without extension? The present, we say, is measured while it is passing, for when it has already passed it cannot be measured, since then it does not exist. But whence and through what and whither does the present pass when it is measured? Whence except from the future? Through what except through the present? Whither except into the past? But this is to say that it comes from that which does not yet exist, through that which has no extension, into that which exists no longer. That this is a serious difficulty is evident from the fact that whenever we measure time it is intervals possessing extension that we measure. But where is the interval in which we measure time that is passing? We can hardly measure it in the future, because while it is in the future it does not yet exist. If it is suggested that we measure time in the present through which it passes, we return to the difficulty already mentioned that we cannot measure that which is without extension. The past, finally, like the future, does not exist, and we can hardly measure that which is no longer in existence.

After commenting (chap. 22) that time appears to be clear and intelligible to us in our constant use of temporal expressions, and yet we must still discover what time is, St. Augustine informs us (chap. 23) that he once heard a learned man say that the motions of the sun, moon, and stars are really the same as "times." [7] Thus St. Augustine leaves for the moment the dilemma at which he has arrived, namely, that time can be measured only in the present, and yet the present has no extension. He hopes that in approaching the problem from a new angle he may be able to discover a solution. To the view that time is constituted by the motions of the heavenly bodies he did not, he tells us, give his assent, because there seems to be as much reason for saying that the motions of all bodies constitute time. If the heavenly bodies should cease from their motion, but

[7] This is decidedly reminiscent of Plato, although there are later writers who also say something similar.

a potter's wheel should continue to move, there surely
would be time by which we could measure the revolutions
of the wheel and say that each revolution required the same
amount of time as the others, or, if the speed of the wheel
varied, that some revolutions required a greater amount of
time than others. And when we were saying this we should
surely be speaking in time and some syllables in our words
would be long and others short, and this would be so only
because the long syllables had sounded during a longer
space of time than the short syllables. The stars and con-
stellations of heaven move in such periods of time as days
and years, as the Book of Genesis says, St. Augustine admits.
One could not maintain that the revolution of the little
wooden wheel was a day, but on the other hand one could
not deny that this revolution in some way represented time.

In this way St. Augustine indicates that he is not primarily interested in what we mean by any period of time,
such as a day or a year, marked off by the heavenly motions,
but rather in the nature of time itself, by which we measure
the motions of bodies and say that one motion is, for example, twice as long as another, even though in so doing
we may not bring into our reckoning the standards provided by the heavenly motions at all. With this in mind he
proceeds to show more clearly that there is no intrinsic
connection between time as such and the motions of the
heavenly bodies.

If we consider a day (including in the day the nocturnal
hours), in which the sun makes a complete revolution from
the east back to the east again, we may ask whether the day
consists in the sun's motion itself, or in the interval of time
in which the motion is completed, or in both. If the motion itself is the day, then there would be a day even if the
sun completed its journey in the space of time that we call

an hour. If the interval of time in which the sun now completes its journey is the day, then there would not be a day if there were only the lapse of an hour between one sunrise and the next, but the sun would have to make twenty-four revolutions in the course of a day. If the day consists in both the motion and the interval of time that this motion requires, then neither one alone would be a day, neither the motion of the sun, if it should be completed in the course of an hour, nor the lapse of time that the sun is accustomed to require for a complete revolution, if the sun should cease from its motion. St. Augustine says, therefore, that he is not trying to discover what a day is, since that is not the essential point, but rather what time is. Using time as a measure we should be able to say that the sun completed its revolution in half its usual time if it did so in twelve hours instead of twenty-four. Comparing these two intervals of time we could say that one was double the other, even though the sun completed its revolution now in one interval, now in the other.

It is interesting to note that St. Augustine does not even consider the person who says that time is constituted by the motions of the heavenly bodies to mean that time is pure motion, because such a notion is repugnant to what he feels about time. He takes this suggestion to mean that all intervals of time, among which are days and years, are dependent for their existence on these heavenly motions, just because we happen to use these motions to mark off certain intervals in the course of time. But he indicates that even if these motions were to cease there would still be intervals of time by which we could measure other motions, such as that of a potter's wheel. While the interval of time in which the revolution of this wheel is completed would not be called a day, as is the interval in which the sun completes a revolution, still there is some interval of time represented in its motion, and St. Augustine even conceives the possibility that we might be able to recognize that a certain number of these revolutions of the wheel would take place in the interval of time that we now call a day, even though the sun's motion had ceased.

This possibility is brought out in his discussion of what we mean by a day. He shows that the interval of time that we now call a day would exist and be intelligible, if not practicable, even if the sun completed its revolution in a shorter interval of time, such as an hour. He does not try to decide whether we apply the term to a certain interval of time for its own sake, as it were, or because within that interval there is one revolution of the sun, and there is no reason why he should, since in our practice the two are generally accepted as identical. The distinction would assume practical meaning only if the sun should complete its revolution more rapidly or less rapidly. If it should suddenly happen that the sun moved twenty-four times as rapidly as it does now, we should then have to decide, St. Augustine implies, whether that new interval would be called a day or the interval in which the sun had formerly completed a revolution. He considers this point important here only insofar as it indicates that time itself is not changed by the motions of the heavenly bodies, even though a temporal expression like "day" might be used differently if there should be a change in these motions.

### AUGUSTINE AND ARISTOTLE ON THE FUNCTION OF THE SOUL

We should observe in this discussion the growing importance of the soul's activity in St. Augustine's conception of time. It is the soul of man that measures intervals of time, as we saw previously, and motion by means of time. The soul has the power to measure intervals of time in which heavenly motions now take place even if those motions themselves should cease or change their velocity. In this view of time there is more than a hint of what we saw in Aristotle, who also considers the activity of soul to be necessary for the existence of time. But St. Augustine's view demands that the soul's activity be considered of primary importance in any discussion of time, whereas the soul, though necessarily implied in Aristotle's entire treatment of time as a number of motion, enters into his discussion explicitly only very briefly and with no attempt to conceal its irrelevant character. For Aristotle time is an aspect of motion, an aspect that exists only insofar as it is perceived by the mind, to be sure, but nevertheless an aspect that can be considered in its relation to motion without explicit reference to the mind that perceives it.

Thus Aristotle speaks at length of the way in which time and motion are reciprocal measures of each other, whereas St. Augustine thinks of the soul as the instrument by which time is measured and by which motion is then measured in terms of time. This gives the soul more independence of external motion than it has in Aristotle, for whom time and motion are the things that measure and are measured, with the soul only an intermediary depending completely upon motion in order to measure time, if he should speak of the soul measuring time at all. For St. Augustine, however, it is the soul, not motion, that measures time, although he would not deny that the motions of the heavenly bodies provide convenient landmarks, as it were, for charting the course of time.

This discrepancy between the two views of time has a consequence that would be of interest in more recent discussions of time. If all observable motions could be thought of as attaining greater velocity, then this would involve a change in time that would remain unperceived to Aristotle, because time is only an aspect of motion. This comment, as a matter of fact, would have no especial relevance within the Aristotelian framework, because the uniformity of time depends upon uniform motion, and there can be no change in time because it is of necessity always in the same relation to motion, and in this relation it has its existence. The relevance is apparent only when we compare St. Augustine with Aristotle. For St. Augustine, if we could conceive of all motions as going faster (and he could admit this more readily than Aristotle, for whom such a statement would hardly have much meaning), we should still be able to say that time had not changed in any way, since time is not an aspect of motion and has some kind of existence apart from its relation to motion. Moreover, it would be evident to the mind that these motions had changed their velocity, because now the mind has been set up as something absolute and independent of external motions in one of its activities, by which it measures time. Although St. Augustine has not thus far told us exactly what time is, it is possible to judge that it involves an activity of the soul and is, moreover, something absolute in relation to which motions can be said to proceed more or less rapidly, any motion and all motion.

Guitton speaks of an absolute time by means of which St. Augustine "permet de concilier la multiplicité des temps locaux avec l'unité de la conscience." [8] This view of a multiplicity of times seems to be based on a somewhat faulty interpretation of the foregoing passage in the author, since time seems rather to be some activity of the soul that is absolute with reference to motions, not to other times.

[8] *Op. cit.*, p. 185.

But, as has been indicated, there is a sense also in which time is absolute for Aristotle, since the relation of time to uniform motion does not change. Since there is no activity of the soul mentioned by Aristotle capable of surveying motion and measuring it with a time that is completely independent of motion, there remains nothing with reference to which time could change for Aristotle. When it is said, therefore, that a greater velocity on the part of bodies would have to involve a change in time for Aristotle, a change, however, that he would not be able to perceive, this could only be said from a point of view such as that of St. Augustine, for whom all motion could be judged in accordance with an absolute standard.

### TIME AS RELATED TO THE SOUL'S ACTIVITY

Not unimportant, perhaps, in suggesting to St. Augustine that time is independent of the motions of the heavenly bodies, though we can hardly call it the chief reason, is the scriptural account of the sun's standing still while the victory was gained (chap. 23). Although the sun was not in motion the battle was completed in a period of time that was sufficient for it. Thus St. Augustine comes to think that time is some kind of distention (*distentio*), since the battle, for example, took place in time. This statement, which he is not yet able to explain further, fits in very well with the conviction previously expressed that time is measured while it is passing, for this would apply to a distention, but there is still the difficulty that the only time that exists is an indivisible present.

Since St. Augustine has already indicated in several places that we measure motion by means of time, it is not unexpected when he declares (chap. 24) that time is not the motion of any body whatsoever, just as he has shown that

it is not the motions of the heavenly bodies. The reason for
this is that the measure must be different from the thing
measured. This sounds somewhat Aristotelian, but actually
St. Augustine on this point is nearer Plotinus, because, as we
saw, St. Augustine considers that time, the measure of motion, is some absolute standard outside of motion. For Aristotle time and motion differ in aspect with reference to a
numbering soul, but are the same in substrate. They differ,
however, in substrate for St. Augustine because time is some
kind of distention manifested in the activity of the soul.
On the other hand, this activity of the soul is not the same
for St. Augustine as for Plotinus, because time as an activity
of soul for Plotinus is the cause of motion in the sensible
universe. It is this motion which is relative to time for
Plotinus, since it depends on time for its constant progress,
and time is an absolute standard for motion as it is manifested to us by motion and employed as a measure when it
has been itself measured by motion. For St. Augustine,
however, motion does not depend on time for its existence,
but time is only the measure of motion. In this respect he
is, of course, more like Aristotle.

St. Augustine states that we estimate the precise length
of time required by any motion only by a comparison with
the time of some other motion, and without such a comparison we are only able to say rather vaguely that a certain
time was long. (Thus we might say that a motion continued for two days, referring the time of this motion to the
motion of the sun.) Although time itself is an absolute
standard for St. Augustine, our use of time when we attempt to be precise in our speech demands that we employ
expressions that are relative, usually, no doubt, to the time
marked off by the heavenly motions, since they provide the
most convenient point of reference. We may remark again

that St. Augustine's conviction that time is to be thought of as an activity of the soul precludes saying that this activity is measured by motion. Aristotle would insist that time is measured by motion as well as motion by time, whereas St. Augustine believes that time is a completely active measure that first measures certain regular and manifest motions and then other motions with reference to these. There is a kind of harmony here between St. Augustine and Plotinus in that both agree that time has within itself no differentiation whereby to provide a basis for the concrete temporal determinations that we are accustomed to make. But for St. Augustine time is that activity of the soul by which motion is measured, while for Plotinus it is the activity of soul by which motion exists.

By virtue of making time something substantially distinct from motion St. Augustine is now able to offer a different way of measuring rest from that of Aristotle. If a body moves and comes to rest intermittently, we are able to measure its rest as well as its motion, and say, for example, that it remained at rest as long as it had previously been in motion, or twice or three times as long as it had been in motion. Although he admits that sometimes we merely estimate these intervals of time instead of calculating them exactly, St. Augustine does seem to think that the mind has the power to measure a period of rest independently of any contemporaneous motion. The independence of external motion that the soul possesses in this respect is in full accord with what he said previously about the mind's capacity to judge that even a heavenly motion, fundamental in our calculation of time, has changed its velocity. Aristotle would say that some motion is necessary to enable us to measure rest, which is the privation of motion, and even the activities of the mind that is attempting to measure the rest would offer a possible, though perhaps not an accurate, means of calculating a period of rest.

Thus, while Aristotle, the student of nature, would consider the mind's activities along with other motions that are measured by time, and omit consideration of that particular activity by which the mind measures, St. Augustine, with his introspective approach, exalts this activity to a position of eminence and from this height surveys the external world of motion as something that is subject to altogether different laws of operation. Plotinus, like St. Augustine, says that rest may be perceived to be in time independently of motion. But this means that an object at rest manifests the life of soul, in which it exists, though not so well as an object in motion. The mental process by which this life is manifested to us constitutes our perception of time, but time itself is something distinct from our perception. But for St. Augustine the object at rest or moving does not manifest time as independent of our perception; time is in the measuring of the object's rest or motion by the mind.

In finding that time is not the motion of any body whatsoever we have also discovered something of its relation to motion and to rest, and now we must proceed (chap. 26) to examine with more precision under what conditions time is to be thought of as the measure of motion. St. Augustine declares that we should not be able to measure motion by means of time unless we were also able to measure time. We must therefore strive to discover how time is measured by us, and this knowledge may very well bring us closer to a discovery of what time itself is. Someone might suggest that time is measured by time, a longer time by a shorter time, just as a longer space is measured by a shorter which is accepted as a unit of measurement. Thus in measuring the time required for the reading of a poem, the time of the entire poem is measured by the time of the individual verse, this by the time of the foot within the verse, this in turn by the time of the syllable, and finally the time of the long syllable by the time of the short syllable. But we are in error if we think that in this way we have arrived at an ultimate and certain measure of time, because the time of the shorter unit can be prolonged so as to become longer than the time of the longer unit, which can also be shortened in pronunciation. Thus St. Augustine is led once again to say that time is a kind of distention, but now he adds very significantly what he has been previously implying, that it seems to be a distention of the soul itself.

In making time a distention of the soul, St. Augustine has made the soul the standard which is absolute and to which motions are referred in order to be measured. The soul is autonomous *qua* measuring and independent of the laws to which external motions are subject. It is difficult to point out the full extent of St. Augustine's variation on this point from Plotinus, because the latter says so little of the individual soul's activity in the perception of time. For Plotinus time must be measured, as for St. Augustine, in order that motion may be measured. But it is an objectively existing time that is measured by motion, although this measurement of time and motion must involve a subjective perception on the part of the individual soul, a perception that Plotinus says demands memory, but about which he says almost nothing else. He is clearly interested in the metaphysical, not the psychological aspect of time. If he were asked how we could be sure that time itself and our perception of it remain constant, he could reply that our metaphysical analysis shows us that the activity of soul does not change in giving the universe its motion, and the motion of the heaven, which provides the best measurement of time, is uniform because it is directly motivated by the life of soul. Moreover, from the standpoint of our perception, we must remember that the individual soul has a sympathy with the nature of soul as such — and with all souls — that brings about a harmony between time itself and our perception of it. Thus there is a constant balance between time, the heavenly motions by which time is manifested, and the life of the individual soul that perceives time. For Plato there is a similar harmony between time as manifested by the motions of the heavenly bodies and the perception of time that is effected by analogous motions within the individual soul. But he too says little about the psychological implications of this perception.

Aristotle insists that time, in order to measure motion, must itself be measured by some regular motion. To St. Augustine this would seem to be going in a circle without the possibility of recourse to some ultimate standard. It is saying that a longer time is measured by a shorter time, which in turn is measured by some regular motion. But how do we know then that this motion is regular and that the time measured by it is consequently of the same length on different occasions? If time is only an aspect of motion why does not time have certain of the characteristics of motion, such as "faster" and "slower"?

St. Augustine's answer to such questions would be that there is a distention of the soul to which all motion is referred, an absolute standard that is able to judge whether motions are faster or slower, even the ones that we are accustomed to use as points of reference. Aristotle, however, would simply say that our analysis of motion and time indicates that we actually employ time in the measurement of motion; this makes it clear that time is uniform while motion need not be uniform. The ultimate justification of this

for Aristotle is in the physical order, since the uniform motion of the first heaven is the reason for the continuity and
uniformity of time. Since the ultimate reason for St. Augustine is in the psychical order, we see that Aristotle cannot
have an absolute standard in the same sense.

All motion for St. Augustine is referred to the soul for its
time. For Aristotle all motion is referred to the motion of
the heaven, and this includes psychical motion, such as the
activity by which we calculate time. Since the heavenly
motion is the ultimate uniformity in the physical order, and
since, further, all motion somehow derives from it, there
results the harmony between time and motion in the physical order that is relevant to the Aristotelian approach. It is
beside the purpose of Aristotle to inquire into the mental
process by which we perceive time, because whatever the
situation is in the physical order we must necessarily conform our minds to it. Even if the first heaven could conceivably change its velocity with reference to some motion
that we do not perceive, this would not affect our perception of time in the physical order because there would remain the same proportion that now exists between this
motion and all other physical motions. This motion must
be uniform since it is ultimate and all other motions are
contained in it and calculated in terms of it.

### HOW THE SOUL MEASURES TIME

In saying, however, with St. Augustine that time is a
distention of the soul, we can perhaps in this way explain
how time is extended; but even then we are obliged to ask
how an indivisible present is to be measured, if the past and
future do not exist, and how an indivisible present is to be
reconciled with a distention. We saw previously that we do
not measure past and future time, and in order to measure

present time it must be passing so as to have some kind of extension in the present — although we did not explain how such an extension might come about. But now (chap. 27) this view must be subjected to critical examination.

It would seem that a sound, for example, cannot be measured before it exists or after it exists because in neither case is there anything to be measured. If this is true it will have to be measured while it is passing, because then it will have some extension in time and not an existence in an indivisible present. But if we measure this sound we must measure it from its beginning to its end, and we cannot do this while it continues in existence. We must therefore wait until the sound is finished in order to measure it; but then we are apparently measuring something that no longer exists. Thus we find that our difficulty is greater than ever. We cannot measure past and future time, because they do not exist; present time, because it is indivisible; passing time, because it is not complete. In the drama of St. Augustine's search for time he has reached the climax, the point where the various threads of his thought achieve their greatest complication. Yet in this very complication there is implicit the end of his search, and the resolution of the drama is rapid.

If we take a verse, such as that from St. Ambrose's evening hymn, *Deus creator omnium*, we say that four short syllables alternate with four long syllables. Our sense perception tells us that in measuring a long syllable we do so by means of a short syllable, saying that the one is twice as long as the other. But if we measure a long syllable by means of the short syllable which has preceded it, the short syllable must have ceased to exist in order for the long syllable to have begun. Moreover, the long syllable itself must have ceased, for otherwise it would not yet be complete. Thus

we cannot measure one syllable with the other unless both
have ceased to exist and are no more, and yet we say that one
is twice as long as the other. St. Augustine now comes to
the conclusion that we do not measure the things themselves,
because they are no longer, but rather something that
remains fixed in the memory.

We must say, therefore, whatever the consequences, that
it is in the soul that intervals of time are measured. But it
is the impression that passing events leave in the soul that we
measure; this impression is present, while the events themselves are past and cannot be measured. This impression is
what we measure when we measure intervals of time.
Therefore, we must say that intervals of time are to be
accepted as identical with this impression, or otherwise we
cannot say that we measure intervals of time. To make
this clear St. Augustine gives us some examples. If we measure a period of silence and say that it was as long as a previous sound, we must measure in our mind the sound as if it
were now passing and refer the time of the period of silence
to the time of the sound as we now recall it. We are able,
moreover, to traverse in the mind poems and verses and dis-
courses even when no one is speaking them, and compare
the time of one with that of another just as if they were
being spoken. Finally, suppose that a person wants to utter
a sound that is rather long and determines through his premeditation how long it is going to be. He traverses a space
of time in silence and, having commended it to his memory,
he begins to utter the sound, which continues to sound until
it has reached the premeditated end. More accurately, we
should say that it has sounded and will sound, for one part
of it is past and the other future. That which is present is
the soul's attention, which transforms the future into the
past, and as the sound is traversed the past increases at the

expense of the future, so that eventually the future is entirely consumed and the sound is completely past.

What St. Augustine says here of silence and sound offers an interesting complement to his previous discussion of the way in which we measure rest as opposed to motion. Just as we can measure silence by means of a preceding sound, so, as we saw previously, we can measure rest by means of a preceding motion. But in order to do this we measure the period of silence by simultaneously measuring the sound as if it were still in existence, and we measure the period of rest by simultaneously measuring the motion as if it were still in existence. While St. Augustine might say that motion and sound are more manifest than rest and silence, and for that reason provide a better standard of measurement, it seems likely that for him rest and silence could also be standards of measurement for their contraries, and that a period of rest or of silence could provide a standard for another period of rest or of silence. This would be in accord with his emphasis on the power of the mind, which measures through its own activity and uses external motion and rest only as convenient points of reference. Aristotle would say, however, that time is the number of motion, and of rest only through motion as an intermediary. But he could explain in his own terms what St. Augustine appears to explain much differently. The very activity by which the mind measures rest, or silence, which is a kind of rest, would be the motion of which time is the number, and through which time could also be applied to rest of any kind. The reason for this, as we saw, is that Aristotle is concerned with the physical aspects of time, and the activity of the mind is merely another kind of motion, for the purpose of his analysis.

St. Augustine, however, distinguishes between the physical and the psychological, and his introspective approach leads him to think of time in psychological terms. This difference of approach, in addition, makes St. Augustine attribute to the mind greater powers than Aristotle would probably be inclined to do. For the latter the mind would be dependent on external motions in order to calculate time with any accuracy, whereas St. Augustine seems to think that independently of external motions the mind is an accurate arbiter of time, although he probably would not deny that some experience is necessary for the attainment of this ability.

By the use of three examples St. Augustine has indicated that it is the mind that measures intervals of time and these intervals are only in the mind. We measure a period of silence by holding in the mind a preceding sound that itself no longer exists and cannot in itself provide a standard of measurement. The silence and the sound have an interval of time capable of measurement only in the mind, which retains some kind of impression of them when they themselves have been completed and no longer exist. Similarly, in the second example, we are said to measure sounds and motions that no longer exist, but which have a duration of some sort in the mind by virtue of which they can be measured. Finally, a person can utter a sound in accordance with a predetermined standard that remains in the mind, and he will bring this sound to an end when the impression of it that his mind is measuring accords with the premeditation that is still in his memory.

In this third example, however, we begin to consider with greater precision how time is in the mind, for the time of this sound is able to be measured only insofar as it is present in the soul. The sound has two parts, the past and the future, since there can be no sound, just as there can be no motion, in an indivisible present. In this indivisible present there is only the attention of the soul by means of which the future becomes the past. When the person who is uttering the sound realizes that the constant diminishing of its future has made it entirely past, he has then measured it in accordance with his preconceived standard. But this diminishing of the future, which as such does not exist, and the increasing of the past, which exists no more, is possible only in the soul, because the soul is somehow not only present, but also past and future (chap. 28).

The soul it is that anticipates the future, attends to the present, and remembers the past. Thus the future does have an existence in the soul's anticipation, and the past in the soul's memory. The present, to be sure, is without extension, but the soul's attention endures, and this attention, because it endures, offers a passage for the future into the past. What we mean by a long future, therefore (this question is finally answered), is a long anticipation of the future, that is, an anticipation of much that is still to pass through the soul's attention; a long past is similarly a long memory of the past, that is, a memory of much that has already passed through the soul's attention. Thus the life of man is distended, as it were, into the future by anticipation and into the past by memory, and both of these are included in the present life of man along with the present attention which is at once the boundary between past and future and the means of passage from future to past. This applies to any time, however short or long it is, even to the whole period of human existence upon earth.

### AUGUSTINE AND PLOTINUS

By means of the metaphor by which the soul's activity is called a distention, St. Augustine has explained the various attributes that time possesses, paradoxical as these seem to be.

The soul has its existence in an indivisible present, but it has the power of distending itself, as it were, in two directions, into the future by means of anticipation, and into the past by means of memory. Since time is to be thought of as a measure of motion, it can exist only in the soul, because only in the soul can there be the simultaneous existence of present, past, and future through which duration can be measured. Since the present in which the soul exists and measures is indivisible, we must not think of the distention which time is called as having a quantitative extension. Rather it is a vital activity that is without quantity, and time, strictly speaking, is without quantitative extension because any duration is measured in an indivisible moment by the coincidence in the soul of past, present, and future. Thus time may be called a distention and said to possess extension with reference to the motions that are measured by it. Since a motion cannot take place all at once and therefore must have a succession within itself in order to exist at all, the soul must represent this succession to itself by means of an activity that can be called by analogy a distention. So the quantitative extension of motion is known to the soul as an extension and can be measured as such only insofar as the soul represents this extension to itself by means of an impression or an activity that is a vital and inextended image and measure of the motion itself. The concept of a vital yet inextended distention enables St. Augustine to reconcile the indivisible present with the fact that time is usually thought of as passing in an extended succession.

There is an interesting parallel between Plotinus and St. Augustine on the relation of time to the soul. Plotinus thinks of the activity of soul as being in itself without succession or extension, but time is extended because it is not this life in itself but rather this life considered from the standpoint of the motion in the sensible universe which constantly and uniformly receives this life. Permanent endurance of the soul is necessary as the reason and source of the succession that is in time, and the relation between the soul and time is an example of the one and the many, or the permanent and the changing, which play such an important part in Plotinus' whole philosophy.

St. Augustine differs insofar as time for him is not the cause but rather the measure of motion. This is due, as we saw, to his disposition to examine time from a psychological point of view, and this must necessarily be from the standpoint of the individual soul. But even as the measure of motion time must have a foundation and reason that is permanent. This is to be found in the soul, whose attention endures amid the successions of motion that are presented to it. But since the time of St. Augustine, unlike that of Plotinus, is essentially a measure of motion, this permanent attention must coexist in an indivisible activity with an anticipation of the future and a memory of the past. These two aspects of its activity are due to the fact that the soul has been placed in a world of change, and, as in Plotinus,[9] time may be said to be a kind of distention when it is considered from the standpoint of change or motion, though insofar as it is an activity of the soul it does not have quantitative extension. Despite the parallel, however, there is a fundamental difference in that Plotinus is seeking a time that has a metaphysical existence independent of any process of measuring, and St. Augustine is searching introspectively for a time by which we measure the duration of motion.

---

[9] iii. 7. 11. 41, διάστασις οὖν ζωῆς χρόνον εἶχε . . . .

### AUGUSTINE AND ARISTOTLE ON THE NOW

Aristotle says that the now, which is not a part of time but rather the boundary of time, gives time its continuity. This now is thought of by Aristotle as the boundary of a continuum, since time is dependent for its existence on motion, which is in turn continuous by virtue of the space over which the motion takes place. Thus time is the measure of motion in a quantitative sense, and the now is a boundary of time and gives time its continuity by modifying a quantity, not unlike a point on a line. Aristotle's view, of course, implies that two nows can be compared by the numbering mind, and this must mean that they are somehow present in the mind together. But this consideration of the psychological aspect of time is not relevant to Aristotle's approach in the *Physics*, where he is concerned with motion only so far as this is due to the activity of nature as a whole.

For St. Augustine, however, the now which is the boundary of time is the present attention of the soul, for time itself exists only in the activity of the soul. This present attention is the boundary between future and past, that is, since his time is psychological, between the soul's anticipation and memory; and this attention provides time with its continuity because anticipation must pass through attention in order to become memory, and thus a link exists between future and past. But this continuity cannot be considered quantitative in the same manner as the time of Aristotle. For the moment at which time is reckoned, from a psychological point of view, must be indivisible, and all the nows that are included in the reckoning must be present to the soul in this same indivisible moment. Thus the continuity possessed by time for St. Augustine must, strictly speaking, be without quantity, although the duration of any motion which is measured by time is thus represented as quantitative. Both philosophers, therefore, may speak of time as the measure of motion, but the measure for Aristotle is quantitative, just as is the thing measured, while for St. Augustine it is a vital activity that is without quantity, but to which quantitative terms may be applied because of that which is measured by it.

Aristotle says that the now may be considered always the same and always different, different because motion, of which time is number, exists in succession, the same because the now is that phase in the motion's progress that exists, so far as it is numerable, and as that which exists it provides the link between that which does not yet exist and that which exists no longer. For St. Augustine the soul's attention is always present and as such it is always the same. But if it were the same in every respect, we should then be considering not time but eternity. So he says that if the present were always present and never went into the past, this would be eternity, not time. In order that the present exist as time it must tend to become nonexistent.

His later discussion, however, shows how this is to be correctly understood. Since the soul exists in a world of change, not everything can be the object of its attention, since motion and change exist in succession. Because of this succession, the soul must use its powers of anticipation and memory as well as that of attention. Thus its attention varies insofar as there is succession in the motion measured by the soul, and attention must therefore transform anticipation into memory in order that the motion may be measured. In this way only does the present become the past, namely, as that which is the object of attention becomes the object of memory. Likewise, that which is the object of the soul's attention exists for the moment and then no more.

But this merely indicates that the terms "past," "present," and "future" are to be understood not in the usual sense but with the refinements added by St. Augustine's examination. They are usually given an application that joins them too closely with motion instead of that which measures motion. The psychological approach shows us that past, present, and future time exist in the soul, although motion does not exist all at once. Thus the permanent now for St. Augustine is not the existing phase of motion so far as this is numerable, as it is for Aristotle, but rather the attention of the soul conceived as a quasi-boundary between the soul's anticipation and memory.

Time, therefore, is in the soul, but the soul is not in time, because its attention always remains attention and never becomes memory. In this St. Augustine follows Plotinus, although the statement that the soul is not in time would have a different meaning for Plotinus. For the latter time is an intermediary between motion and that which, while unmoved, is the cause of motion. For St. Augustine time is between motion and the soul which measures motion by existing as something relatively permanent in a changing universe.

### TIME AND THE UNIVERSE

Time is in the soul, but it is the universe of changing things that is in time, insofar as the succession which the universe requires for its existence is capable of being perceived and measured by the soul. This is the metaphysical aspect of time, and it enters frequently into the philosophical discussions of St. Augustine. In fact, the context in which he explains time is devoted to an exposition of the account of creation in Genesis, and his purpose is to show how the universe is in time, while God the Creator is in eternity.

Since the universe, therefore, cannot exist all at once but must exist in succession, it may be said to be in time, and time cannot exist unless there is a universe in which motion exists, a motion which is capable of being measured according to shorter and longer intervals by a mind.[10] Thus time demands both a universe of motion that does not exist all at once and a mind that is somehow apart from this universe and is able to grasp in an indivisible moment various phases of this motion and to measure its duration.

There are certain mysteries about the beginning of time, but, difficult as it may be for the mind to understand how time has a first moment, he is assured of this by Scripture, which tells us that every creature had a beginning, and it is clear that time is a creature as well as the universe whose motion time measures and the mind of man which does the measuring. Since time is inconceivable apart from the universe, we must not think of God as existing in a temporal priority to the universe. "Nullo ergo tempore non feceras aliquid, quia ipsum tempus tu feceras." [11] Even if the universe had had no beginning, however, still it would not be co-eternal with God, because time necessarily involves change and succession, whereas God exists immutably in eternity, which is an unchanging present. "Et nulla tempora tibi coaeterna sunt, quia tu permanes; at illa si permanerent, non essent tempora." [12] For when we look at time

---

[10] Corresponding to the soul's distention is the succession in motion that is due to the fact that motion cannot be simultaneous. See *The City of God* xi. 6, quis non videat, quod tempora non fuissent, nisi creatura fieret, quae aliquid aliqua motione mutaret, cuius motionis et mutationis cum aliud atque aliud, quae simul esse non possunt, cedit atque succedit, in brevioribus vel productioribus morarum intervallis tempus sequeretur? Cf. Étienne Gilson, *Introduction à l'étude de saint Augustin* (Paris: Vrin, 1929), pp. 250–252, for some helpful remarks on this subject.

[11] *Confessions* xi. 14.

[12] *Ibid.*; cf. *The City of God* xii. 17.

in its metaphysical aspect, we see that there is a succession of phases in motion which may be called metaphysical instants or nows insofar as they are capable of being the object of the soul's attention.

Thus time has in itself a progression from the metaphysical point of view, and this progression makes it impossible for any time, however long, to be co-eternal with eternity.[13] The relation between time and eternity is difficult to grasp, because we tend to think of eternity in a temporal way, despite the fact that the perfect and immutable substance of God, Whose duration is eternal, has no succession within itself and exists complete in the indivisible, perfect, and ever complete present of eternity.[14] We can say that although eternity does not precede time in a temporal way it is prior to time as its cause, and unless eternity existed there would be no time, just as there would be nothing created if God did not exist in eternity.[15]

We have seen that the soul's activity must be superior to the universe of motion in order to measure it, and be something relatively permanent from the standpoint of the flux and succession of this motion. Since time exists in an indivisible activity of the soul, it can be called a distention, not in a quantitative sense like the motion that it measures, but metaphorically with reference to the quantitative distention of motion. But however figurative this distention may be in contrast with the distention of motion, the fact that the soul is in a universe of change and is able to grasp succession not all at once but piecemeal, as it were, signifies that in con-

[13] Cf. *ibid.* 16.
[14] Cf. *Confessions* xi. 13.
[15] *Ibid.* i. 6, summus enim es et non mutaris, neque peragitur in te hodiernus dies, et tamen in te peragitur, quia in te sunt et ista omnia: non enim haberent vias transeundi, nisi contineres ea. Cf. *De Trinitate* ii. 5. 9, ordo quippe temporum in aeterna Dei sapientia sine tempore est.

trast with God's eternity the life of the soul on earth is a real distention. God's knowledge of the universe is without distention of any kind, for the entire course of time is known to Him at once, whereas the soul of man is obliged through the threefold activity of anticipation, attention, and memory to participate somehow in the flux of motion itself. Thus in contrast with the utter simplicity of God's knowledge man's perception of motion and the measuring of it that we call time are in a flux: ". . . . expectatio rerum venturarum fit contuitus [elsewhere called *attentio*], cum venerint, idemque contuitus fit memoria, cum praeterierint: omnis porro intentio, quae ita variatur, mutabilis est, et omne mutabile aeternum non est." [16] Thus the soul's activity, which must be permanent with reference to motion in order to measure it, and which possesses an *attentio* that endures, is nevertheless in flux when contrasted with the perfect and complete permanence of God.

### TIME AND THE LIFE OF MAN

The whole life of man is a distention because of the necessity to grasp the succession of motion in piecemeal fashion, and also, from a moral point of view, the diversity of interests which attract the soul and make life a distention in a somewhat different sense of "distraction": "ego in tempora dissilui, quorum ordinem nescio, et tumultuosis varietatibus dilaniantur cogitationes meae, intima viscera animae meae, donec in te confluam purgatus et liquidus igne amoris

---

[16] *Confessions* xii. 15. Though the activity by which the soul measures motion must be superior to the succession of motion, which is in time, St. Augustine is also aware that some activities of the soul are subject to temporal succession; see *De Genesi ad Litteram Liber Imperf.* 3. 8, quae [anima vel ipsa mens] utique in cogitationibus movetur, et ipso motu aliud habet prius, aliud posterius, quod sine intervallo temporis intelligi non potest.

tui." [17] The twofold distention of the life of man makes it difficult to grasp eternity and is in large measure the reason for the tendency of men to think of eternity in a temporal fashion.[18] Only through a better knowledge of God Himself will the soul be able to avoid the errors of those who conceive God as if He existed in time, but the complete emancipation of the soul from the distention and distraction attendant upon life in this world must wait for the vision of God in the life to come.

There is in St. Augustine a hierarchy similar to that of Plotinus but with important differences. The soul for St. Augustine is in a sense midway between God and the sensible universe. The soul has received its existence from God, but the universe does not proceed from the soul in which time exists, for St. Augustine is speaking of the individual soul whose activity is called time because it measures motion, not because it is the cause of motion. Time is a distention for both philosophers because of its relation to motion: for Plotinus, because motion is produced by soul's activity, which is accordingly said to be extended, for St. Augustine, because motion is measured by time. Since Plotinus, however, is speaking of the nature of soul as such, he is more inclined to insist that its nature in itself is eternal, while it may be called temporal only insofar as it communicates motion to the universe.

St. Augustine sees a distention in the very activity of the soul because the soul he is speaking of is the individual soul that measures motion through its activity of attention, anticipation, and memory. But the soul is able, through the

---

[17] *Confessions* xi. 29.
[18] *Ibid.* 11, quis tenebit illud [cor hominum] et figet illud, ut paululum stet et paululum rapiat splendorem semper stantis aeternitatis et conparet cum temporibus numquam stantibus et videat esse inconparabilem. . . . ?

grace of God, to attain a stable contemplation of eternal being by withdrawing from its existence in a universe that forces it to participate in the motion around it. Soul for Plotinus, however, is not separated from eternity as is the individual soul for St. Augustine; but when Plotinus speaks of the individual soul that perceives time he agrees that some kind of spiritual progress is necessary in order that the soul may become truly eternal. Although the soul for St. Augustine is distended, it must possess some kind of permanence with reference to motion in order to measure it, and it is thus superior to the sensible universe although inferior to God's eternity.

Eternity is prior in nature to time for Plotinus and St. Augustine. The latter believes that there was a first moment of time because of Scripture, but he says that even if there had not been a first moment the temporal universe would not be co-eternal with God, just as Plotinus says that eternity does not run along with time, but is indivisible. But Plotinus thinks that time exists necessarily, and the existence of eternity implies the existence of time as its inferior, just as time implies eternity as its cause. Time for St. Augustine, however, like everything created, proceeds from the will of God. It is not implied in eternity, although eternity is necessary to uphold time in existence, just as God's conserving power is required for the continued existence of any creature. For this reason, Plotinus can derive time from eternity as its image, while St. Augustine is obliged to proceed by an empirical examination of time that is similar to Aristotle's, but is psychological rather than physical. But Plotinus, as we saw, did not carry out the implications of the metaphor of image to the extent that Plato did, seeming rather to dwell upon the differences between eternity and time. This is in accord with the descent of soul, with all the moral implications of such a concept; but these differences are primarily due to the fact that one of his favorite devices is contrasting a higher and a lower stage in the hierarchy of being by means of contraries. St. Augustine suggests the metaphor of the descent to describe the soul's position in the universe.[19] This is even more metaphorical, as it were, than Plotinus would think of it, because the existence of the soul for St. Augustine is not implied in any way in God's existence. But it expresses a fundamental moral conception of time that sometimes tends to bring the two fairly close together. It is the obligation of the individual soul to collect itself from the dispersion it suffers in being placed in a universe of change, and in this way prepare itself for the ascent to eternity, an ascent that is implied for Plotinus in the very nature of being, but for St. Augustine is due to the will of God.[20]

Thus the soul is conceived by St. Augustine to be subject to the dispersion of a temporal existence, although his psychological analysis of time itself tells him only that time is in the soul. For Plotinus soul, in which time exists, is not itself in time, whether this be the world soul or the individual soul. But the individual soul has its affections and productions in time, and here time has a moral significance that Plotinus does not discover in the mere derivation of time from eternity. Thus the definition of time that St. Augustine obtains by his psychological approach must be viewed in the context of his whole spiritual life.

[19] Cf., e.g., *ibid*. iv. 16, revertamur iam, domine, ut non evertamur, quia vivit apud te sine ullo defectu bonum nostrum, quod tu ipse es, et non timemus, ne non sit quo redeamus, quia nos inde ruimus; nobis autem absentibus non ruit domus nostra, aeternitas tua.

[20] *In Joannis Evangelium* xxxviii. 8. 10, ut ergo et tu sis, transcende tempus. Cf. *De Genesi ad Litteram Liber Imperf.* 13. 38, . . . ut signum, id est quasi vestigium aeternitatis tempus appareat.

# Conclusion

It seems fairly clear that the problem of time is an entirely different problem for each of the four ancient philosophers whom we have been discussing. The differences in the nature of the problem arise first of all from the fact that each philosopher is looking for a different kind of being, a kind of being that is in accordance with his view of reality as a whole. Moreover, in making this being explicitly clear both for others and, in no small measure, for himself, the individual philosopher utilizes what seems to him to be the proper method of investigating such a problem; and this method bears some analogy to his investigation of any other philosophical problem. Plotinus remarks [1] that we possess a notion (*ennoia*) of time with which our explanations should be in harmony. It is in searching for these explanations that the philosophers diverge, making the search a different kind of problem for each. But a more detailed consideration of the individual philosophers and the contrasts their investigations exhibit should clarify these rather general remarks.

Plato's *Timaeus* is a glowing description of the harmony and beauty of the universe, a hymn of praise, one might almost say, to the manifold evidence of intelligence to be observed in the workings of nature. Because of the motion in it Plato relegates nature to the sphere of becoming, which is opposed to unchanging being. But pure becoming would not account for the order of nature, for order has in

[1] iii. 7. 7. 14–15.

it something of the intelligible, and it is being that is intelligible, while becoming is sensible. It is one of the chief tasks of the dialogue, therefore, to bridge the chasm between being and becoming, that is, to assimilate the realm of becoming, as it is represented in the universe, to that of being. The method by which this is accomplished is the use of a series of metaphors, no one of which need be accepted in its precise literal meaning, which serve to awaken in the soul of the reader an insight into the nature of the universe and its motions that could be produced — for Plato — in no other way. So he warns us time and again that the teaching of the dialogue is only a probable account, a likely story that will serve its purpose even if it is not literally true. Moreover, since words are unstable and shifting, we cannot depend on them to retain the meaning we give them unless we come to their aid. We must fix them as far as possible by setting them in analogies and proportions with other terms, and hope that such relationships will preserve something of their original force.

The first important step in assimilating the universe to intelligible being is the introduction of a soul of the universe, conceived on the analogy of the human soul, with intelligence directing the motions of the universe, even as in us intelligence, which is capable of knowing true being, can direct our actions harmoniously to the attainment of good. But this is not sufficient for Plato. The universe must be likened to true being in a more direct way than through the possession of a soul, which is, after all, not said to be being but only capable of knowing being. Thus we are led to time, which brings the universe into a closer relationship with being because it is a moving image of eternity, one of the most important characteristics of true being. Before time there was only the random motion of pure becoming.

This chaotic condition was as far from being temporal as it was from being the orderly universe we now perceive. All changed with the introduction of time, which as a moving image of eternity renders the motion of the sensible universe harmonious and intelligible. The universe now resembles true being so far as this is possible for anything in the realm of becoming.

The imitation of eternity by time is characterized by Plato in a variety of ways. Most important is his statement that time imitates the perfect unity of eternity by means of a numerical progression. Only true being can possess perfect unity because only true being is perfect and unchanging. Anything other than being must involve multiplicity. The chaotic condition that preceded the entrance of time into the universe (whether this chaos was prior in a chronological way or some other way) was sheer multiplicity and was completely opposed to the abiding unity of true being. If we call being eternal because it is perfect and unchanging, what are we to call this chaotic motion that has not come under the power of mind? Whatever we choose to call it, we must not call it temporal because it is very carefully distinguished by Plato from the universe, which alone is temporal of things that become. The temporal universe holds a middle position between true being that is eternal and sheer becoming that possesses only multiplicity. This middle position is due to the fact that number is midway between unity and multiplicity.

Number is not to be looked upon as sheer multiplicity because it is a collection of units; it is a projection of unity into the realm of multiplicity, an imitation of unity or an assimilation of multiplicity to unity. Thus it is very illuminating to call time an image moving according to number, for number itself is an image of unity, which is the chief characteristic of eternity. Time is therefore placed midway between eternity and sheer becoming, just as number is midway between unity and sheer multiplicity. If, then, we distinguish being and becoming as the intelligible and the sensible respectively, time will contain within itself something of both, because it is a combination of being and becoming. Insofar as time involves becoming, that is, multiplicity, it is an object of sensation; insofar as it involves being, that is, unity, it is an object of thought. It is a projection of the intelligible into the sensible order and is appropriately described in mythical form as the product of a divine intelligence that fashions its handiwork after an intelligible model.

According to the myth time is to be found in the orderly motions of the universe, for these motions guard the numbers of time, and, in fact, are identical with time. These motions of the heaven of fixed stars, and of sun, moon, and planets provide the moving image of eternity that time is said to be. Their motions are in the sensible order, that is, in the realm of becoming. But they have been assimilated to the intelligible order, true being, and their orderly arrangement as time is to be discovered by man's intellect. Each of the heavenly motions, such as that of any planet, when set in relation to the others, gives rise to a set of numbers; thus each of these motions can be called a time, and the whole of time comprises many individual times. When these individual motions complete a cycle and the heavenly bodies return to their original relative position, the perfect number of time is fulfilled. The perfect number of time comprises many numbers, that is, many individual times; in this perfect number the complex and diverse numbers of time achieve their greatest harmony and unity, and most closely resemble therein the unity of eternity. Time consists, therefore, of cycles, or cosmic units, and it is unending. In this way too it is like eternity; since it cannot be eternal it exists in everlasting succession.

In the dialogue Plato distinguishes sharply between space and time. Space existed "before" the universe came to be, whereas time and the universe came into existence together. The processes of becoming took place in space even before they were brought under the influence of mind. Becoming as such demands space, but not time — in the proper sense of the term for Plato. In the universe, therefore, motion in space is sensible; time is sensible insofar as it involves motion in space, but it has an important ingredient of the intelligible in it because it has been fashioned in imitation of eternal being. Time does not arise from space, nor space from time; the two belong to radically different orders. Time cannot be understood in relation to the lower sensible order along with which it exists in the universe, but rather with reference to the higher intelligible order of thought. It represents an upward striving on the part of the universe, an attempt, as it were, to be something more than mere becoming.

Thus we live in a universe that is governed by the harmonious motions of the heavenly bodies, that is, by time, a reflection of intelligible being. No mechanical causes are sufficient to account for the workings of nature; these are merely subsidiary to the real causes, which are intelligible principles operating in a sensible framework. Man, no less than other things in the universe, should be guided by the harmonious order of nature. He receives instruction, both intellectual and moral, in observing and meditating on the plan of the universe. His idea of number, for example, comes from the heavenly motions; and his moral life is set in order by imitating the orderly course of the heavenly bodies. Thus time is a source of moral good for man as well as of physical good for the universe. Its role is to perfect the universe, including man, by introducing intelligibility, goodness, and beauty into the realm of becoming.

For Aristotle in the *Physics*, or in any other of his works, the problem of time is entirely different. There is no need for him to relate time to the entire universe by a series of analogies and metaphors, since he employs terms that have a fixed and literal meaning within a given science. The subject matter of the *Physics* is restricted to natural motion, and the work contains a treatment in orderly sequence of this motion and the various concepts that are related to it. One of the most important of these is time, which is treated only insofar as it can be related to motion. There is no need to construct an entire universe that will contain motion and time in a certain way. In the existing universe motion and time are perceived by the student of nature, and he must analyze them.

Aristotle begins in his usual fashion by setting forth the difficulties connected with time which should be solved by a correct analysis. Then he continues by discussing the problem in a more positive, but still preliminary and dialectical, manner by investigating its relation to motion. The result of this preliminary investigation is the discovery that time is not identical with motion, but is not independent of motion, for when we do not perceive motion we have no perception of time.

Aristotle's positive analysis of time relates it closely to motion and magnitude; this is most obvious in the case of local motion. The motion is continuous because the spatial magnitude that it traverses is continuous, and time is continuous because motion is continuous. So also there is in motion the distinction of prior and posterior, which arises from spatial difference, and this distinction of prior and posterior in motion, insofar as it is numerable, is time. Thus the continuity of time and the succession of prior and posterior in it are founded on motion and ultimately on spatial magnitude. This does not mean, however, that time is to be confounded with motion or magnitude. For time is characterized primarily by the fact that it numbers motion according to prior and posterior. In place, strictly speaking, there is not so much a prior and posterior — since all the parts exist simultaneously — as there is mere difference. Moreover, motion as such is only the actualization of the potential. The prior and posterior in it arises from the fact that the motion takes place over the different parts of the magnitude in succession. Thus motion and the prior and posterior that is in it are the same in substrate, but they have a different definition. Time is the prior and posterior in motion insofar as this is numerable, that is, the number of motion according to prior and posterior. To define time merely in terms of motion would be to confuse time with its substrate; a formal element, namely, the prior and posterior, is necessary to distinguish time from motion, and this formal element must be brought into the definition.

In consequence of the relation of time to motion, time may be called the measure of motion, since time as well as motion is continuous. But from another point of view it may be called the number of motion, since there is in time a sequence of inextended moments or nows that, taken as the limits of the continuous flow of time, provide a series of numbers analogous to an abstract numerical series. Other characteristics of time as well are explained by reference to motion. Time is everywhere in the universe because all things are movable. There is only one time despite the variety of motions because time is the number of motion according to prior and posterior and does not number motion in any other way. That is to say, the now must be one because all existing motions have as number the same now, since, despite their diversity, in respect of prior and posterior they do not differ. Moreover, if time, being continuous and uniform, is to be the measure of all motion, including motions that are intermittent and irregular, it must primarily be the measure or number of a motion that is itself continuous and uniform. This can only be circular motion, as Aristotle indicates at length. Time, therefore, primarily measures circular motion and by means of it measures other motions as well.

In all this discussion time is considered only insofar as it can be related to motion and explained in terms of motion. The question arises in the course of the investigation whether there would be time if there were no soul. Aristotle answers that if time is something numerable there could be no time without a soul capable of numbering, although motion, which is the substrate of time, could exist. With this brief answer the question is dismissed because no further consideration is relevant to the *Physics*, which is interested in time only as it can be analyzed by the student of nature, who can be presumed to possess a numbering soul from the outset. There naturally arises the possibility that time has a psychological aspect as well as the physical, but that cannot be investigated in a context devoted to natural motion and the attributes belonging to it. We may also suppose that time has other aspects as well, such as ethical, but all these can be discussed only in the proper science in accordance with the method proper to the science.

In later sections of the *Physics* and in the other physical works time comes into the discussion, but not in such a way as to make us revise our opinion of the method by which

Aristotle has arrived at his definition of time and the properties derived from that definition. The eighth book of the *Physics* traces all motion back to an unmoved mover and thereby gives us the ultimate cause of all physical motion and, consequently, of time. In another treatise, *On the Heaven*, we are informed that time goes back to the first heaven as its source, with no time existing outside the heaven. These passages, through analysis supplemented by observation of phenomena, instruct us in the ultimate causes and principles that make motion and time what we have already found them to be. They do not affect the definition that was reached at the proper time and by the proper method, but rather give a further explanation that is not included in the bare definition.

In Plotinus time presents still a third problem. This philosopher begins his consideration with a firm belief in the three divine hypostases, soul, intellect, and the One, in ascending order. These hypostases and the general world-view they represent are in large measure a systematization of certain passages in Plato, but this alone is far from explaining Plotinus' view of time or of anything else. They express a view of reality and of philosophical method very different from Plato's. This is evident in Plotinus' treatment of time.

For Plotinus as well as for Plato time is an image of eternity, but in a rather different sense. Whereas Plato emphasizes the mathematical nature of time as image, Plotinus neglects this completely. For him the concept of life is the important one, because time seems to be related somehow to the motion of the universe, which proceeds from the life of soul. Number would have embarrassing consequences for Plotinus, since he cannot reconcile number with the infinity of time. "Life" also offers a convenient means of relating soul to the prior hypostasis, intellect. Since motion is in time, time is prior, because for Plotinus everything "exists in" something that is prior to itself, and ultimately all things exist in the One. Since the universe proceeds from soul, it seems reasonable to him to make time the life of soul insofar as soul is productive of the universe, an effect lower than itself. "Life," therefore, is an effective term from Plotinus' point of view, since it explains how soul is an intermediary between the motion of the universe and intellect, which is the life of thought. The latter is on the same level as eternity, and time, the life of soul, is a lower form of life, but higher than the universe, which receives its motion from this productive life of soul.

As a matter of fact, Plotinus does not stress the nature of time as image. For him everything is a descent from the primal One, and each stage in the process of descent must be differentiated from that which precedes it. Thus there is the tendency for Plotinus to distinguish rather sharply the higher and the lower, very often by means of a pair of contraries. This he does in differentiating time and eternity, the productive life of soul and the life of intellect. He employs such pairs of contraries as change and permanence, continuity and indivisibility, unending succession and self-contained infinity. For this reason the concept of "image" is far less prominent in Plotinus than in Plato, who introduces time in order to assimilate the realm of becoming to that of being, and consequently looks upon time as something that is striving upwards instead of descending. The effect of this difference between the two philosophers may be observed in the moral value that time has for them. For Plato time is a source of order and harmony that man should utilize for his moral life. While Plotinus would not deny the harmonious nature of time (since it belongs to soul), he cannot help regarding it as a lower stage in a hierarchy above which man should ascend. His moral teaching on time, therefore, is that man should go counter to it and rise to eternity, whereas for Plato time in its upward striving is already leading man to eternity.

In accordance with his philosophy of hypostases Plotinus is looking for a time that is in some sense substantial. The statement that motion is in time means for him that motion exists in time as in a cause, and an adequate cause is found in the life of soul. One can readily see why Aristotle's treatment of time is inadequate from his point of view. He would admit that the statements of Aristotle have considerable truth in them; in fact, his procedure in criticizing other philosophers is very much like that of Aristotle. Plotinus' criticism of Aristotle is that he has not found and makes no attempt to find the essential nature of time, but offers an accidental attribute or attributes of time as if they were the essence. In the context into which time enters for Aristotle it must be defined in its relation to motion, in its function as number or measure. That is the reality or essence of time for Aristotle in the role of student of nature. But this is not the manner in which Plotinus considers time, and he does not believe it proper or profitable to consider time from this narrow, functional point of view. He cannot agree that time, in which all moving things exist, is other than substantial. If time were nonsubstantial, what would become of those things that are said to exist in it? He feels that it is beside the point, therefore, to treat time in any other way. It does not seem correct to say that Aristotle and Plotinus differ in their account of time because Plotinus has a world soul. The difference is rather one of method, since Aristotle's definition of time would be the same even if the ultimate cause of time for him were a world soul.

Aristotle's approach to the problem characterizes time in terms of motion and space (though this is immediately clear only in the case of the time of a local motion). There is a sense in which Plotinus also does this. For the life of soul, being eternal, is in itself without succession; it can be said to possess succession only on the analogy of the motion which is produced by it. So if time is called changing and successive in contrast to eternity, that is really because its effects are produced in succession in the universe, and time is therefore characterized in terms taken from motion and space. But there is the very important difference that time precedes and causes the spatial order for him. Soul's productive life, which is time, is at such a level in the hierarchy of being that its effects must be in motion and in space. Thus the cause is described in terms of the effect whenever contrasted with its own superior in the hierarchy. But, whereas Aristotle speaks of time in a purely physical way, Plotinus insists that it is a vital activity which, though characterized in terms of its effects, nevertheless transcends them and is something different.

Plotinus, like Plato, does not give a definition of time, at least in the Aristotelian sense of "definition." But he can approximate a definition because of the hypostases which he has, but which Plato has not. In the hierarchy of being — which flows without interruption from the One — intellect and soul are given positions that, while not completely fixed, are at least relatively the same; and so with other things, including soul and the universe. Time can thus be given a position in the hierarchy that bears a relation to other things. But it cannot be fixed in the precise manner in which an Aristotelian definition would do this. For the hypostases themselves are capable of shifting somewhat, and other terms, such as "life," are most variable. When, therefore, Plotinus calls time the "life of soul actualizing one thought after another," or something of the sort, this can be accepted only as an approximation of an Aristotelian definition. For in one sense the life of soul cannot have successive actualizations; its activity can be so characterized only with reference to its effects, which do come into existence in succession.

With St. Augustine the psychological view of time comes to the fore. Aristotle had hinted that time has a psychological aspect, but he dismissed it as irrelevant to his purpose. There is in Plotinus more than a hint of his interest in the psychology of time, but the actual details that he offers are few. His teaching might be called, with qualification, psychological in the sense that time is an activity of soul. And indeed St. Augustine's view bears much resemblance to that of Plotinus. But Plotinus' view is metaphysical rather than psychological, because for him time exists independently of the perceiving soul. His statement that memory must be employed in order to perceive the flow of time anticipates St. Augustine's emphasis on the role of memory. But the latter has a full-fledged psychological view that, despite its antecedents, emerges as something entirely distinctive.

For St. Augustine, as for Aristotle, time is the measure of motion, but in a different way. For Aristotle time is a physical measure that possesses many of the characteristics of the motion that it measures. But St. Augustine removes time from the realm of the physical and places it in the soul of man, where it exists in an entirely different manner. Time is an activity of the soul by which man measures motion. This activity has a threefold aspect insofar as it considers motion as past, present, and future, namely, memory, attention, and anticipation. Outside the soul, strictly speaking, nothing exists except the present phase of motion, which is indivisible. If motion, then, is to be considered continuous and measured as such, this can only be done in the soul, which has the power to bring together past, present, and future in one indivisible activity of its own.

Thus time is in a different order of things from motion. It is not physical; it is not really quantitative or extended. It is rather an activity of the soul used by man as an instrument for the measurement of motion in the physical, extended universe. There is no little resemblance to the teaching of Plotinus, who also thinks of time as a vital activity, not really possessing extension in itself. But for St. Augustine the purpose of this activity is the measurement of motion; for Plotinus time is rather the cause of motion and is not essentially a measure, although it may be used as such. St. Augustine thinks of time's function in a more Aristotelian manner. As a matter of fact, many of Aristotle's statements about time can be readily translated into the psychological doctrine of St. Augustine. This can be done the more readily because the latter permits time to be described in physical terms on the analogy of the motion it measures, even though in itself it cannot be called physically extended in any way. It is interesting to note that the original difficulties presented by Aristotle are taken up by St. Augustine at various points in his discussion. His answers to these difficulties are in psychological rather than in physical terms. For example, past and future time, which appear to be nonexistent, exist in the soul's memory and anticipation. The now, which is ever present for Aristotle as the existing phase of motion insofar as it is numerable, becomes for St. Augustine the attention of the soul, which forms a boundary, though not a physical one, between past and future, that is, the soul's memory and anticipation.

This psychological view of time is closely connected with

St. Augustine's moral views. The soul must use time, not because of any intrinsic necessity, but because it has been placed in a universe of change and succession. It must distend itself, though not in a quantitative manner, into past and future by means of memory and anticipation, because the objects of its knowledge do not persist but come into existence in succession. The concept of "distention" easily leads St. Augustine to think of this life as a distention or distraction in the moral sense; the soul is somehow dispersed by existing in a world of this kind. It must gather itself by God's grace from this dispersion and rise to a higher form of life. At the same time it can hope to rise to a contemplation of God, which will remove it from the distention involved in a temporal existence.

One last question might be raised with regard to the four philosophers under consideration, especially Aristotle, Plotinus, and St. Augustine, namely, whether they have been more successful than later philosophers in distinguishing time from motion and space and, in general, in offering a satisfactory solution to the problem of time.[2] For Aristotle time depends on motion and place, the two of which may be said to have a prior and posterior insofar as they provide the foundation for the prior and posterior in time, motion by its order and succession, place by spatial difference. To the objection, such as Kant might offer, that the order and succession in motion presuppose time, Aristotle would doubtless say that time in *his* sense as "number" presupposes succession in motion,[3] and that, if one finds it

---

[2] Questions of this kind have been raised, and rightly so, by Clark in his stimulating article, *op. cit.*, pp. 351–358.

[3] The statement of Ross, *op. cit.*, p. 65, that for Aristotle time is the *ratio essendi* of motion is hard to understand. As a consequence, Aristotle's declaration that time depends for its existence upon the soul he finds unsatisfactory and dismisses lightly, *ibid.*, p. 68.

difficult to consider the succession in motion as being in itself nontemporal, the reason is the mind's natural tendency to number the succession it perceives, that is, to consider it in a temporal manner.[4]

With St. Augustine it might seem at first glance that to define time in terms of expectation and memory is to use terms that themselves involve time. But regardless of the temporal implication of these terms, St. Augustine, like Aristotle, attempts to give time — that is, the measuring activity of the soul — a basis in the succession of motion itself and thus avoid circularity. The metaphorical distention of the soul corresponds to a real distention of motion.

Plotinus applies temporal terms to the creative life of soul because this is time only when considered in relation to the motion which is caused by it. This creative life of soul, which is in itself nontemporal and nonspatial, produces its effects in temporal succession as well as with spatial differentiation because these effects are on a lower level of reality which is characterized by greater multiplicity.

Although none of these views, therefore, may be expected to answer every question about the relation of time, motion, and space that has occurred to later philosophers, yet if they are understood in relation to the purpose each philosopher had in mind and to the specific philosophic method of each, they would seem neither to be circular in setting forth the nature of time nor to involve "a surreptitious passing from space to time."[5] There is still much opportunity to evaluate the contributions of these four philosophers in the light of subsequent developments in the history of thought,

[4] On the ease with which Aristotle considers that we perceive time, see *On Sense* 448a19–30.

[5] Clark, *op. cit.*, p. 352, refers especially to Aristotle and Plotinus, but he admits that, in addition to them, "everyone else seems to be impaled on the horns of a painful dilemma."

but that is a large task and one that is beyond the scope of the present work.

Thus time, which was treated metaphorically by Plato as the moving image of eternity, physically by Aristotle as the number or measure of motion, and metaphysically by Plotinus as the productive life of soul, receives at the hands of St. Augustine a new facet, the psychological, and emerges from ancient philosophy a well favored but still provocative problem.

# SELECT BIBLIOGRAPHY

# Select Bibliography

Aristote, Physique. Texte établi et traduit par Henri Carteron. 2 vols. Paris, 1926, 1931.

Aristotelis De Caelo Libri IV. Recognovit D. J. Allan. Oxonii, 1936.

Aristotle on Coming-to-Be and Passing-Away. A revised text with introduction and commentary by Harold H. Joachim. Oxford, 1922.

Aristotle's Metaphysics. A revised text with introduction and commentary by W. D. Ross. 2 vols. Oxford, 1924.

Aristotle's Physics. A revised text with introduction and commentary by W. D. Ross. Oxford, 1936.

Augustine, The Confessions of. Edited by John Gibb and William Montgomery. Cambridge, 1927.

Augustini, Aureli, S., Confessionum Libri XIII. Edidit Martinus Skutella. Lipsiae, 1934.

Augustini, Aurelii, Sancti, Episcopi, De Civitate Dei Libri XXII. Ex recensione B. Dombart quartum recognovit A. Kalb. 2 vols. Lipsiae, 1928, 1929.

Baeumker, Clemens. Das Problem der Materie in der griechischen Philosophie. Münster, 1890.

Baurain, Liévin. "Le temps d'après saint Augustin," Revue augustinienne, I (1902), 183–193.

Bröcker, Walter. Aristoteles. Frankfurt a. M., 1935.

Carteron, Henri. "Aristoteles de Tempore," Bulletin de la Faculté des Lettres de Strasbourg, III (November, 1924), 28–40.

Clark, Gordon H. "The Theory of Time in Plotinus," The Philosophical Review, LIII (1944), 337–358.

Cornford, Francis M. Plato's Cosmology. The Timaeus of Plato translated with a running commentary. London, 1937.

Duhem, Pierre. Le système du monde, I, II. Paris, 1913, 1914.

Gent, Werner. Die Philosophie des Raumes und der Zeit. Bonn, 1926.

Gilson, Étienne. Introduction à l'étude de saint Augustin. Paris, 1929.

Gotschlich, E. "Aristoteles von der Einheit und Verschiedenheit der Zeit," Philosophische Monatshefte, IX (1873), 285–290.

Guitton, Jean. Le temps et l'éternité chez Plotin et saint Augustin. Paris, 1933.

Heath, Louise R. The Concept of Time. Chicago, 1936.

Heinemann, Fritz. Plotin. Leipzig, 1921.

Leisegang, Hans. Die Begriffe der Zeit und Ewigkeit im späteren Platonismus. Münster i. W., 1913.

Levi, Adolfo. Il concetto del tempo nei suoi rapporti coi problemi del divenire e dell'essere nella filosofia di Platone. Torino, 1920.

Martin, T. H. Études sur le Timée de Platon. 2 vols. Paris, 1841.

Philoponi, Ioannis, in Aristotelis Physicorum Libros V Posteriores Commentaria. Edidit H. Vitelli. Berolini, 1888.

Platonis Opera. Recognovit Ioannes Burnet. 5 vols. Oxonii, n.d.

Platonis Timaeus Interprete Chalcidio cum Eiusdem Commentario. Recensuit Ioh. Wrobel. Lipsiae, 1876.

Plotin, Ennéades. Texte établi et traduit par Émile Bréhier. 6 vols. Paris, 1924–1938.

Procli Diadochi in Platonis Timaeum Commentaria. Edidit Ernestus Diehl. 3 vols. Lipsiae, 1903–1906.

Simplicii in Aristotelis Physicorum Libros IV Priores Commentaria. Edidit Hermannus Diels. Berolini, 1882.

Sperling, Karl. Aristoteles' Ansicht von der psychologischen Bedeutung der Zeit. Marburg, 1888.

Taylor, A. E. A Commentary on Plato's Timaeus. Oxford, 1928.

Themistii in Aristotelis Physica Paraphrasis. Edidit H. Schenkl. Berolini, 1900.

Thomae Aquinatis, Sancti, Commentaria in VIII Libros Physicorum Aristotelis (Opera Omnia, II). Romae, 1884.

Torstrik, Ad. "Über die Abhandlung des Aristoteles von der Zeit, Phys. Δ 10 ff.," Philologus, XXVI (1867), 446–523.

Verwiebe, W. Welt und Zeit bei Augustin. Leipzig, 1933.

Wunderle, Georg. Die Lehre des Aristoteles von der Zeit. Fulda, 1908.

Zawirski, Z. L'évolution de la notion du temps. Cracovie, 1936.